From Killer to

Common Cold:

Herd Protection and the

Transitional Phase of Covid-19

DAVID M. GRAHAM, MD

Editing & Design: Zachariah DeGiulio
Additional Editing: Emily Perlmutter Kamen

ISBN: 9798688753523

To My Twins

who taught me to write between diaper changes.

CONTENTS

1 HOW A VIRUS VIEWS THE WORLD

A virus, yet again, changed the world. A bag of protein and genetic material intent on making copies of itself has been unleashed on humans.

SARS-CoV-2—the virus responsible for causing Covid-19—isn't even a living thing. A virus is just a tiny collection of proteins and genetic material wrapped in your own cellular membrane with one goal: to make more copies of itself.

This killer virus jumped from bats into humans, rapidly traversing the globe in the respiratory secretions of an interconnected planet. Yet, since the introduction of animal domestication, human pandemics from viruses have been relatively commonplace. These human pandemics have shaped our shared histories.

Consider a virus like smallpox. Once a common cause of childhood death and disfigurement, evidence of this virus has been found on mummified remains from ancient pharaohs. Waves of this viral pandemic wiped out vast numbers of humans, from European royalty to entire Aztec and Inca civilizations. Smallpox influenced politics in Europe and decimated the native populations of the New World, allowing settler colonialism to flourish. There are multiple examples of pandemics every century, and now, after a one-hundred-year hiatus, another pandemic virus is upon us.

Although viruses are not living, it might be helpful to consider viruses like SARS-CoV-2 as if they lived, breathed, and walked, just like us. What if we were to walk a mile in the shoes of SARS-CoV-2? How does a virus see its human host? What inherent restrictions do viruses have, and how do human cultures shape those restrictions? Can we learn something about Covid-19 by thinking about how a virus experiences the world?

The interaction between humans and viruses is complicated. Anthropomorphizing viruses allows us to think beyond the week- or month-long pandemic planning horizons that governments use. On one side, there is a virus that evolves and modifies the rules of the game while in progress. On the other side, we humans strive to understand the rules, anticipating what changes (both for us and the virus) are inevitably in store. One thing is clear—this virus, SARS-Co-V-2, will change people around the globe.

Human culture is built upon identifying problems and organizing people to create solutions. Where we live in the world drastically affects how we experience Covid-19. We all have different social norms, political gambits, and ever-changing attitudes towards the virus. Culture affects the way we see Covid-19.

Moreover, many have struggled to learn the science of virology and epidemiology through the lenses of political, social, and economic concerns. We are seeing the messy give-and-take of the scientific process in action, occurring simultaneously with haphazard policy proposals. Too often during this pandemic, policymakers endorse a solution now, only to scorn the same solution later. The political response to the pandemic feels like constructing your parachute after jumping off the plane.

Individuals, on the other hand, deal with viruses differently, both physiologically and through their personal decisions. We all have slight variations in our immune systems and underlying health, which massively differentiates our experience of Covid-19, both for ourselves and our family members. Our personal experience with the virus shapes both the way we view what individuals can do now and what we should expect in the future.

Instead of focusing on the rapidly changing political and scientific landscape for bites and bytes of information, what if we instead profiled Covid-19 like we were profiling a criminal? Let's line up all the usual suspects! Who (or what) has done something like this before? What can we learn by looking at prior pandemics, and, more specifically, at the family of coronaviruses that already infects humans? We might not be able to sentence our culprit (or cure it for that matter), but we can hopefully learn enough about Covid-19 to predict parts of its behavior and know what to expect in the next few years and beyond.

Profiling depends on homology and behavioral consistency. Homology, the idea that similar crimes are committed by similar offenders, allows us to look at other pandemics and consider how Covid-19 is different. Can we learn something from the crimes of smallpox and influenza that might inform us about the future of Covid-19? Behavioral consistency speaks to the idea that an offender's crimes will be similar in nature. We know there are seven other human coronaviruses currently in existence. Can we look at the crimes of the other coronaviruses and figure out what to expect with Covid-19?

Rather than using the give and take of scientific progress to predict the future of Covid-19, what if we used what we already know about evolution and virus/host interactions to make future inferences? As we build the scientific evidence base to better understand Covid-19, is there a way to know now, in advance, how it will all end? Yes.

I believe the destiny of SARS-CoV-2 is already written. With or without a vaccine, with or without an effective treatment, with or without expected technological advances, we are destined to interact with this virus forever. Only a major paradigm-shifting development of the future—something truly out of left field—will rid this world of Covid-19.

This book is not so much a tale of science on the ground today. The science is changing too rapidly to consider writing a book on that topic. Instead, this is a tale of evolutionary biology and the natural limitations placed on viruses, humans, and the co-evolving cultures each group simultaneously creates. Within those limitations, we know that SARS-CoV-2 is not eradicable and will become endemic.

There are already four coronaviruses that are endemic and cause the common cold. Endemic means that they circulate widely, at all times, and in low levels in human populations throughout the world. SARS-CoV-2 will become the fifth endemic human coronavirus. Believe it or not, the process of a coronavirus becoming endemic has already happened at least once before in our written history.

Even though we cannot eradicate Covid-19, it will be less lethal in the future. This is predictable either through evolution of the virus itself or through changes in its host. Humans, our immune systems, or our cultures will change the face of this killer disease so that it resembles the common cold.

Pandemics and infectious diseases have killed more people and shaped human history more than any other aspect of nature. We have been in an arms race with infections since the beginning. Until the twentieth century, infections killed more soldiers at war than human enemies did. We are, and have been, in a constant struggle against infections for millennia, though we forget this when only looking back over our own lifetime. Hygiene, clean water, antibiotics, vaccines, and good old public health have changed the nature of infectious diseases in modern society.

Although there are still many places on earth where infectious diseases are the number one killer of young children, diseases of civilization such as heart disease and cancer have overtaken infectious causes of death in wealthy countries. The impact of infection on our daily life has faded. It has been over one hundred years since the last truly devastating pandemic plagued us. We forgot. We did not plan, and deaths and disabilities from Covid-19 are the inevitable and unfortunate consequences of not preparing for the usual suspects to return to their old, criminal ways.

This will be a short book. Using basic virology and evolutionary biology, I aim to convince you that Covid-19 will become endemic no matter what humans do. We will need to learn to live with this virus, and I hope to show you how to do so.

We'll start by reviewing some basic science about viruses and how they interact with hosts. Next, we will look at influenza and discuss some prior pandemics, contrasting influenza to the family of coronaviruses that already live in and among us. Once we have a basic understanding of viruses (the usual suspects), we will learn a little about epidemiology, viral replication dynamics, and herd immunity. From this, I will demonstrate how eradication of SARS-CoV-2 is unlikely and discuss how the next few years may play out. Covid-19 infections will continue during what I call the "Transitional Phase," as we progress from epidemic to endemic. Finally, we will review how a current common cold coronavirus, OC43, went from epidemic to endemic during our written history.

Covid-19 is here to stay, but rather than drinking from the fire hose of ongoing scientific discovery, what can we learn from a review of science theory? We have evidence and probable cause. It is time to prosecute SARS-CoV-2 and understand the fallout from the crime. Instead of looking at statistics, modeling, and the ongoing messiness in medical journals, let's look at history to see potential futures.

2 WHAT DOES A VIRUS WANT?

Viruses are explosive.

They are an aggregation of proteins and genetic material with a single goal—to make more of themselves. Some viruses literally blow the cell they are trapped inside up in order to escape. When given enough resources, they demonstrate exponential, explosive growth. Remember that viruses, unlike bacteria, protozoa, and fungi, aren't even alive. They are the ultimate parasites that require a living organism—often you—to survive and reproduce.

SARS-CoV-2 is the virus that causes the disease Covid-19. The "CoV" stands for coronavirus, which is a large family of closely related viruses that cause various illnesses in many different species. We will learn about the human coronaviruses in chapter 4, but first, we'll discuss what exactly a virus is and how it interacts with its host.

Viruses are small—much smaller than even bacteria. They are the ultimate minimalists, carrying only what they need to get from one host to another. They must do three basic things. First, they must transfer from host to host via the environment. Then, once in a host, they need to spread from cell to cell. In the cell, they make copies of themselves.

Viruses take over the metabolic machinery of a cell and then make so many copies of themselves that they obliterate the cell. Next, they find another cell to infect. Within a host, only the host's immune system can break this chain of cell-to-cell transfer.

Surviving in the environment outside the host, however, is difficult. The virus must leave a host (usually via sneezing, coughing, or diarrhea) and get onto, and then into, another host. The environment is a hostile place for viruses. They are diluted by space and time and desiccated by sunlight. If they land on the wrong type of host, it is all for naught. A virus only infects one species of animal.

To protect themselves from the environment, enveloped viruses use a lipid membrane to coat themselves. Not infrequently, viruses actually use your own cell's lipid membrane to do so. Smart! They use your cellular machinery to replicate, and your cell's membrane as a coat. They are minimalists, but not ideal houseguests.

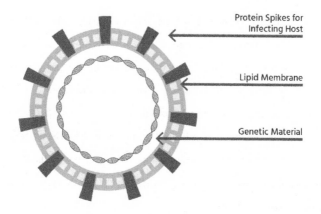

Image adapted from "Why Soap Works" by Jonathan Corum and Ferris Jabr, New York Times, 3/13/20.

Next, there are little protein spikes that stick out of the virus and latch on to your cells. The proteins that stick out of coronaviruses look like the solar corona on electron micrographs, hence the name. The protein spikes attach like a lock and key to receptors of your cells. These receptors are there for some other functional purpose, but the virus learns to take advantage of them in order to gain entry. A virus attaches protein spikes to your cell's receptors, allowing it to enter your cell. Once inside, the virus hijacks your cellular machinery and uses it to make copies of itself.

Viruses have either RNA or DNA as their genetic material. RNA viruses mutate more rapidly and can possess some extra proteins to replicate. We can sometimes target those extra proteins with medications, which make RNA viruses slightly more treatable.

Coronaviruses are large, enveloped RNA viruses. They are found in many different animal species and cause different syndromes in different animals. Cows and pigs get diarrhea from their versions of coronavirus, whereas other species can have respiratory, neurological, and asymptomatic illnesses.

Humans are exposed to animal coronaviruses all the time. However, as the virus is adapted to living in its host species, a great majority of the time it cannot attach to human cells. It takes a mutation in the protein to allow it to bind like a lock in key to the new host's receptors.

SARS-CoV-2 likely started in bats, but we are still not entirely sure. The ancestor of SARS-CoV-2 could cause a cold, diarrhea, or no symptoms at all in bats. Then, randomly, a mutation happened in the spike proteins in the ancestor virus that allowed the virus to spread from bats to humans. This step may actually have happened through an intermediary—a third animal species. The mutation allowed the spike protein of SARS-CoV-2 (which used to only latch onto bat cells) to latch on to human respiratory cells. From this random mutation in a bat coronavirus, the pandemic began.

So, a genetic change in the spike protein occurred in SARS-CoV-2 which allows it to bind to human respiratory cells and enter those cells. Once inside, it uses our cells' reproductive machinery to make more of itself. These copies then are released locally and infect other local cells. There is exponential growth until the virus runs out of resources, or the immune system halts the growth. Remember, SARS-CoV-2 wants to spread to new hosts so it can infect others and continue to make copies of itself. In order to facilitate spreading to a new host, the virus causes symptoms. Symptoms, such as coughing or sneezing spray the virus into the environment where it may attach to a new human's respiratory cells, continuing the epidemic process via person-to-person spread.

Viruses that mutate and jump species from animals to humans are called zoonotic viruses or zoonoses. Usually, humans are dead-end hosts, as the virus isn't able to spread from person to person. It is difficult for a virus to learn how to bind a new receptor, replicate in a new species, and spread efficiently. This is why pandemics are relatively rare, even though humans get exposed to animal viruses all the time. However, when a virus does jump to humans and can efficiently spread from person to person, watch out world.

The immune response to this is complex, to say the least. The immune system is, perhaps after consciousness, the most complicated concept in medicine. Each individual has a slightly different immune system, but each of us have specific and non-specific responses. The non-specific response is pretty easy to picture, as you have experienced it many times. When your body is worried that something is going on, perhaps an invader is on board, it dumps out cytokines and other immune-modulating molecules as the initial phase of host defense. You feel faint, fatigued, hot, sweaty, tired. This is all your body's way of saying, "Hey, get ready!" Fever is part of the non-specific host defense response. Your cells tolerate higher body temperatures more readily than the invaders. This non-specific response primes your cells for a fight and may ward off an initial infection. Usually, a non-specific response gives your cells a fighting chance to defend themselves and prepares your body for the specific immune response. There are other non-specific proteins and defense mechanisms as well, but they're less relevant to viral infections.

After a few days, your body processes the virus and makes specific antibodies against viral proteins. Antibodies are produced by B-cells and are one arm of specific immunity. Antibodies can be detected in blood tests. The antibodies coat the spike proteins of the viruses and prevent them from attaching to new cells. If you have them, it usually implies you are immune to the specific infection. In reality, it is a little more complicated than that. For example, HIV easily survives outside of cells even when there are plenty of antibodies. In addition, anti-coronavirus antibodies wane over time and may or may not protect you from future infection. When considering coronavirus infections, immunity due to specific antibodies is usually neither permanent nor long lived.

In addition to antibodies, the cellular immune system is another component of the specific immune response. The cellular immune system destroys your cells infected by a virus. To simplify, there are different T-cells that orchestrate your cellular immune system. Some T-cells detect your cells that are infected and kill them, stopping the production of more virus. Other T-cells are the actual conductor of your immune orchestra. Finally, memory T-cells remember that you have been infected in the past and respond rapidly when next you encounter a similar virus.

The immune system is full of moving parts and is unique for every person. We all have slightly different immune systems that may be better or worse at fighting off different infections. A question to consider now, which will be answered later: Might there be some people in the population who are better than others fighting off Covid-19, just by random chance?

The relationships between viruses and their hosts are complex. In nature, invaders and hosts come to a common understanding over time. In its native species, a viral infection is frequently mild or even asymptomatic. In general, only when a virus initially jumps species does it tend to cause widespread death and destruction. After all, that is what an epidemic is: a new infection that causes massive amounts of death and destruction. Remember, the goal of a virus is to make more copies of itself. A dead host is a dead-end host—no more copies of the virus. A more efficient way to transmit usually implies a mild illness, which allows ample opportunity to spread to other hosts. A virus wants to be benign, because usually that is the best mechanism to replicate and spread.

That a virus wants to make more of itself is a tautology—it is true because it is true. If the virus didn't make more of itself, it wouldn't be here to make more of itself. It wouldn't exist. We, in turn, wouldn't know it existed and therefore wouldn't bother to ask why it exists.

In the end, replication is what all lifeforms "want." Understand that this is not a conscious desire, rather a just-so story This tautology is a basic principle of evolutionary biology. A replicating element replicates. That's why it is here to observe. This is true for all replicating organisms or lifeforms.

Evolutionary biology is the study of change over time in replicating elements such as humans and viruses. In infectious diseases, we see evolution in real time, as bacteria learn how to become resistant to antibiotics, or HIV learns to become resistant to the therapy we prescribe. In humans, the effect of evolution is quite a bit slower. We actually see human behavior affect evolution more than changes in our genetics. But evolutionary biology is a complex story for a different book.

In the survival of the fittest, the fittest Covid-19 virus is the one that makes the most copies of itself. Certainly, we will see genetic changes in SARS-CoV-2 that affect its ability to replicate. Evolutionary biology can help humans and SARS-CoV-2 both reach our goals. Through behavioral modifications, humans can suffer and die less from infection, and SARS-CoV-2 can evolve to reproduce itself more. Believe it or not, as a novel host to SARS-CoV-2, humans need to help, rather than hinder SARS-CoV-2 to reach its goal. A benign virus is a good virus.

3 INFLUENZA & PANDEMICS

We can learn a lot about pandemics by understanding influenza. While Covid-19 and influenza are by no means identical, comparing, and especially contrasting, these two respiratory viruses will help us better understand the ongoing Covid-19 pandemic.

Influenza is a remarkable respiratory virus, first-in-class for causing seasonal *and* pandemic outbreaks. We worry about influenza every respiratory season. Any time people get sick during this time—from a runny nose to an upset stomach—folks often say they have the flu. There are many different types of respiratory viruses, however most people mistakenly identify influenza as the cause of the flu. I like to say: If you feel like you got hit by a truck, then it might be influenza.

We follow the progress of seasonal influenza as it usually starts down south in the warmer states. Then, like a wave, we see cases increase gradually from south to north. Positive tests increase rapidly until epidemiologists announce: Influenza is here. At that point, most mild-to-severe respiratory illnesses that present to emergency rooms are influenza. There is usually a bump in cases as folks gather for the holidays and spend more time gathered indoors. Then, cases fade away as spring takes hold.

These yearly influenza waves, however, are just the remnants of past pandemic influenza viruses. The 1918 influenza virus, for example, circulated as seasonal influenza for a few decades, only to disappear and be replaced by other strains. It reemerged as the H1N1 swine flu epidemic in 2009 and has been causing seasonal misery ever since. Even though we have vaccinated against this H1N1 strain yearly since 2009, it continues to cause death and disease every respiratory season. Strains come and go depending on the immunity levels of the host population.

Influenza is one of the greatest viruses of all time in terms of its ability to escape the immune system. There is no other respiratory virus in its class. Every year, influenza changes a little. This antigenic drift involves minor mutations that affect how our immune system recognizes influenza. We often see in advance that drift has occurred, and we try to change the influenza vaccine every year to match the predominant circulating strains. Sometimes we guess right, but sometimes an antigenically different strain circulates, causing the vaccine to perform poorly. Generally, 20-50% efficacy is expected from seasonal influenza vaccination.

With SARS-CoV-2, don't expect the equivalent of antigenic drift to happen. Even though all RNA viruses are susceptible to accumulating mutations, there are scant examples that suggest coronaviruses mutate and escape the immune system. The difficulty lies in the need to change the spike protein so that the immune system no longer recognizes it, while the virus maintains the ability to attach to cellular receptors in order to enter the cell. It is possible that SARS-CoV-2 could have a mutation that escapes immune detection yet still binds the cells in the respiratory tract, but this type of antigenic drift is not a common feature of coronaviruses. It is likely we will see different strains of SARS-CoV-2, but less likely that these will entirely evade the immune system. At the very minimum, there should be some cross reactivity or partial immunity to any drifted strain.

Instead of drifting to evade the immune system, the problem with coronavirus is that immunity to it is not long lasting. In 6-24 months, despite having a perfectly adequate initial immune response, you might get the same virus again as your immunity wanes. Thus, drift is not the issue with relapsing Covid-19 infections, but rather, loss of immunity.

Immunity to influenza, on the other hand, can be extremely long lasting. In fact, when H1N1 returned in 2009, those who had it when it last circulated in the 1960's were usually still immune. Thus, the elderly, despite their weakened immune systems due to normal aging, were relatively protected from H1N1. Unlike coronavirus, influenza may evoke long-lasting immunity after infection.

While antigenic drift causes seasonal influenza as the virus slowly mutates over time, antigenic *shift* causes pandemics of influenza. Antigenic shift is a major genetic change that usually involves the reassortment of influenza from another animal species. There are non-human animals that carry influenza— most commonly pigs and birds. What if human and bird influenza strains co-infect a pig simultaneously and the virus recombines? The pig might start producing humanized bird strains of influenza. These recombinant strains pass back to a human, and if effective human-to-human transmission occurs, a new influenza pandemic begins.

Antigenic shift is reflected by the H and N monikers of influenza. For example, H1 and H3 correspond to human pathogens currently, while H5 and H7 correspond to bird pathogens. The N can be different as well, as in N1, or N9. H and N are important functional proteins influenza carries that allow us to specifically identify them. If influenza swaps out its human H1 for a bird one, then a virus for which there is no baseline immunity may be born. If the virus maintains its ability to efficiently spread from human to human, many people get infected with a novel virus all at the same time.

Fortunately, most cases of recombined humanized-bird

influenza do not effectively spread from human to human. If a new strain jumps into a human, we see a few cases in people exposed to animals, but they don't pass it on. These viruses fail somewhere in the chain: either in cell-to-cell movement, making copies in the cell, or in human-to-human transmission.

Humans are exposed to animal coronaviruses all the time. Fortunately, coronavirus pandemics are rare as animal coronaviruses don't bind to human receptors or efficiently transmit from human to human. SARS and MERS (which we learn about in the next chapter) are examples of a non-human strain of coronavirus that learned to infect humans by passing through an intermediary species. Similarly, SARS-CoV-2 is the result of a bat coronavirus that likely passed through an unknown intermediary animal and learned how to infect humans. Just as importantly, SARS-CoV-2 knows how to spread efficiently from human to human.

Influenza makes these jumps regularly via antigenic shifts. It mostly circulates during winter in the Northern Hemisphere, but it never truly goes away and occasionally pops up in the summer. In the Southern Hemisphere, influenza peaks during their winter (the North's summer), so we often get a sneak peek into what our influenza season holds. Influenza spreads and multiplies in cold conditions with low humidity, especially when people are packed indoors. This seasonality provides a relatively straightforward way for Northern scientists to develop vaccines, as they can look at the Southern Hemisphere and try to predict what will spread north for the winter. Vaccination for influenza is inexact; frequently, the vaccine is not as good as we hope. This is due to drift, as different strains than expected circulate. In addition, vaccination is not effective for everyone. More often than not, the elderly struggle to produce antibodies to influenza after vaccination. Thus, those at highest risk for complications from influenza are often the least protected by vaccination. With Covid-19, this is also the concern. Those most at risk for Covid-19—the elderly and immunocompromised—simply won't respond to Covid-19 vaccines, either.

Despite concerns about effectiveness, the influenza vaccine may be disease modifying, and, perhaps, a Covid-19 vaccine will be, too. That is, you might get less sick from influenza if you get the influenza vaccine. Similarly, if you get a vaccine for Covid-19, you might still get the virus, but hopefully you will be less sick. The disease has been modified to be less severe.

As far as medications go, we have several for influenza, but none for the common cold. Influenza can be lethal. Thus, we tolerate some side effects from the medicines. In general, since viruses use your own cells to reproduce, it is more difficult to find medicines that don't have unacceptable toxicities for viruses. Stated specifically, since a virus uses you to reproduce, we need to find a way to kill the virus without killing you! We tolerate medications for influenza that have significant side effects as they may have more benefits than risks. All medicines, however, have risks. If you just have the common cold, how safe would a medicine have to be in order for lots of people to take it? Is it worth taking a medication with side effects in order to treat a runny nose? After all, we have to worry about all our healthy cells too, not just the ones that are zombie-virus-making machines.

It is likely there will be several classes of medications developed for coronaviruses. The question is not only how effective they are, but also how toxic they are, especially when Covid-19 becomes the common cold.

When considering how to treat influenza, we must also consider what exactly a pandemic is, which is a collection of regional epidemics. This simple definition trips up most media and politicians and leads to bad reporting and policy making. You cannot look at the world as a whole, nor can you even look at a country as a whole, as an epidemic affects different regions differently. In fact, in the United States, it is often not accurate to look at a state as a whole. Populous states such as California and New York have vastly different geography, population density, health care resources, and socio-economic factors, which affect the spread and severity of an epidemic such as Covid-19. Although there has been a call for national- or state-specific policies to address Covid-19, these will not work. The pandemic is not your community's pandemic. It is your epidemic, which comes together across communities to create a pandemic. Only in your community can you act.

So, while a pandemic is a set of simultaneous epidemics

around the world, your regional epidemic is what is important to consider. How is your regional health care and public health system able to address your specific community's needs? What can we do here and now to make a difference? While it is true that we all share resources such as PPE or testing supplies, and infectious disease do not respect lines drawn on a map, interventions either work or don't work in a specific time and place. It is either your local ICU that is full or not full, and your local public health department that has capacity or is overwhelmed. The adage "think global, act local" not only applies to the environment, but to pandemics as well.

Influenza has caused many pandemics throughout human history and provides a solid focus for pandemic planners. Covid-19 threw a wrench in these plans. As compared to influenza pandemics, coronavirus pandemics are not well understood. There are important differences between these viruses, however, and one cannot use an influenza blueprint for a Covid-19 pandemic. Let's now look at human coronaviruses specifically. SARS and MERS are examples of coronavirus pandemics that fizzled out, and we can learn a lot from studying them.

4 HUMAN CORONAVIRUSES AND PRE-EXISTING IMMUNITY

Part of the reason why we know as much as we do about SARS-CoV-2 is because it comes from a large family of coronaviruses that infects many different animal species. Coronaviruses share a common evolutionary past and all diverged from a common ancestor at some point. That said, just as whales and mice are both mammals, despite the similarities, comparisons only work until they don't. Humans host six different coronaviruses of medical importance whose effects vary widely from SARS-CoV-2. We can learn a lot about Covid-19 by examining the other human coronaviruses and seeing how they behave, but we do have to be careful with our comparisons.

We'll start with the coronaviruses that can potentially cause epidemics before we move on to the endemic ones that cause the common cold. Finally, we'll discuss the likelihood that there is some pre-existing immunity to SARS-CoV-2 in humans due to cross-reactive immunity with non-Covid-19 coronaviruses.

The virus SARS-CoV-1 causes Severe Acute Respiratory Syndrome (SARS). Scientists previously called the virus SARS until 2019, when the nomenclature changed to incorporate the virus that causes Covid-19. Thus, we now have SARS caused by SARS-CoV-1, and Covid-19 caused by SARS-CoV-2. SARS caused a pandemic scare in several countries around the world from 2002–04. With a high mortality rate, it killed about 8,000 people, but has subsequently been eliminated from human populations. SARS jumped species from a horseshoe bat and was passed onto humans through an intermediary, the palm civet (a nocturnal weasel-like creature that lives in Asian rainforests).

There are a lot of similarities with the diseases SARS and Covid-19! Indeed, these two viruses are the most genetically related of all the human coronaviruses, and both derive from bat coronaviruses. But why did SARS burn itself out? This is important to understand, because it is for homologous reasons that Covid-19 won't burn out.

First off, SARS makes people really sick. That is, folks usually wind up in the ICU with viral pneumonia and sepsis. There is no asymptomatic or mild form of SARS. Second, SARS is only contagious once people are actually sick. Since you are not worried about asymptomatic or pre-symptomatic transmission, it's a lot easier to do airborne isolation for people with SARS by having people wear those scary isolation spacesuits. In fact, we were so effective at preventing transmission of SARS that is has been eliminated from the human population since 2004. Even though they are genetically very similar, SARS is not a good model to use to in order to understand Covid-19, because it is always severe and easy to contain via isolation.

There is a second non-endemic human coronavirus to consider, Middle East Respiratory Syndrome (MERS). MERS is also known as Camel Flu and is caused by MERS-CoV, which is less related than SARS-CoV-1 and -2 are to each other. MERS also jumped species from bats but now lives in camels. When humans encounter camels who have MERS-CoV, they can become dead-end hosts for the virus. That is, when humans get MERS-CoV, we are an incidental host and don't efficiently spread the virus. The virus spreads well camel to camel, but not human to human.

This is the main difference between MERS and Covid-19. Human MERS is not very contagious, whereas Covid-19 is extremely contagious. When people interact with camels, MERS occasionally pings a human host. When it does transmit from camel to human, it causes a severe illness with up to a 35% mortality rate. Because it lives quite comfortably in camels, MERS will likely never be eradicated. However, it will not cause an epidemic in humans unless it learns how to spread efficiently from person to person. It is not a good model for understanding

Covid-19, because MERS is endemic in camels but a rare zoonotic infection in humans.

Endemic human coronaviruses operate a bit differently. Endemic, again, means always around. So, the endemic coronaviruses, also known as the common cold coronaviruses, are pretty useful to study when trying to understand Covid-19. There are four strains of coronaviruses that are presently endemic in humans. They have delightful names like HCoV-NL63 and HCoV-OC43. The "HCoV" stands for human coronavirus and the letters and numbers after the dash represent the name of the strain. They circulate widely and year-round. In the past, we never paid all that much attention to the four strains of endemic coronaviruses because of their benign omnipresence. If you swab enough noses in daycares at any time during the year, you will find their genetic footprint. They cause asymptomatic infections, outbreaks of the common cold, and may also rarely cause viral pneumonia, especially in those with underlying health or immunity issues.

Coronavirus infections in children are present year-round, but outbreaks occur most commonly in the winter. Some argue that coronaviruses are seasonal (more common during the winter, like influenza) but I think that conclusion is based upon false evidence. Studies that only look for the virus when there are symptoms, not surprisingly, find endemic coronaviruses more common during the respiratory infection season. This is, after all, when folks crowd indoor spaces and share air and viruses more frequently. Studies that look year-round, however, find endemic coronaviruses year-round.

In children, the common cold coronaviruses are commonly co-pathogens. That is, on PCR testing we detect a coronavirus *and* another virus, such as RSV, influenza, rhinovirus, or any number of other viruses we can detect. You frequently find an endemic coronavirus *and* another respiratory virus when you have a child hospitalized with viral pneumonia. In adults, however, especially those with immunosuppression or lung issues, you occasionally see viral pneumonia due to the endemic coronaviruses.

It seems that young children are generally spared from the severe consequence of endemic coronavirus. They may carry it in their nose, are asymptomatically infected, or just have minimal symptoms like a runny nose. When you think about hygiene in daycares, you wonder why the infection doesn't spread to all children. That is, how is it possible that all children don't have the virus all the time? For me, herein lies what is still a bit of a black box, an immunological mystery. There remains an unexplained phenomenon regarding why young children don't frequently get sick from endemic coronaviruses. Children, relative to their exposure and immune status, seem to be spared. This is analogous to what we see in children with Covid-19, where they too seem to be partially spared. This black box is the subject of a future chapter.

Children do build some immunity to coronaviruses. There is relative immunity to each coronavirus strain after exposure, but the immunity wears off over time. In addition, there is cross-reactive protection to different strains. That is, you can have OC43 now and be partially immune to NL63 for a while as well. So, how likely is it that there is partial immunity to Covid-19 from the endemic coronaviruses? It turns out that it is very likely, as we will discuss later. And this is, in general, a pretty common phenomenon with respiratory viruses.

As it turns out, there are lots of examples of partial immunity provided by prior infection from a different viral strain. In influenza, for example, this is exactly the case. If you look at the 2009 H1N1 outbreak, it turns out the elderly were relatively protected from illness caused by this "novel" influenza strain because of their history. These folks had been exposed to the remnants of the 1918 influenza back in the 1960's, before that particular H1N1 strain was replaced by an H2 strain. So, because people had an influenza in 1960, they were protected in 2009 when the H1N1 strain re-emerged as a slightly different strain. That is the power of pre-existing immunity, where your memory T-cells remember that you have had this virus before (or a similar version), and immediately get back to work controlling the virus. So, we know there is pre-existing immunity in endemic coronaviruses and understand that there are correlates in influenza. How can we use that information to learn more about the effects of Covid-19?

Nature Reviews Immunology released a summary of recent immunological studies related to pre-existing immunity and

Covid-19.[1] While I am not otherwise focusing on recent literature, this proof of concept is important to note. This report finds that T-cells react due to SARS-CoV-2, and this was likely due to common cold coronaviruses. In fact, somewhere between 20-50% of people have cross reactive T-cells present prior to any SARS-CoV-2 exposures. It was more common to have the T-cell recognize the components of the virus that the viruses may share in common. This is big news! Somewhere between 20-50% of people have pre-existing immunity to Covid-19! In five different populations around the world, there is evidence that prior infection with endemic coronaviruses primes the immune system to respond to Covid-19.

Maybe this is why children do not frequently get ill due to Covid-19. They are protected by frequent exposure to the common cold coronaviruses. What is also unique about children and coronavirus is that co-infection with other viruses is common if children are symptomatic. This leads to the suggestion that all coronavirus may be less pathogenic in kids than in adults. Specifically, children may tolerate coronavirus infection better than adults.

It may be that common cold coronaviruses are not pathogens at all in children, only co-pathogens. If an endemic coronavirus happens to be living in your nose when you get a bad case of influenza, the test may pick up both when it's really

---

[1] Sette, A., Crotty, S. *Pre-existing immunity to SARS-CoV-2: the knowns and unknowns.* National Review of Immunology (20), 457–458 (2020).

only the influenza that's actually causing disease. So, you might be colonized with one virus, while the clinical disease is due to the bad actor—the pathogen. Certainly, we will learn more about the role of the endemic coronaviruses in human disease over the next few years, but they will play an important role in the Covid-19 pandemic.

Finally, we know these endemic coronaviruses are around all the time but tend to circulate in waves. There may be a common strain this year, but a different strain next year. These waves are believed to be a result of some cross-reactivity between the strains that cause partial, pre-existing immunity to the other strains. The important thing to note about immunity to coronaviruses: it goes away over time. You might have some partial protection from memory T-Cells, but antibodies wane. You can be infected by the same strain of endemic coronavirus again at some point in the future, but it might not be as bad the second time.

It seems likely that asymptomatic children spread common cold coronaviruses. Covid-19 also has a unique quality, as you can be asymptomatic or pre-symptomatic and spread the virus 48 hours before you get non-specific symptoms. That is, up to about 48 hours before you develop non-specific symptoms of an infection, you can be contagious. This is a major aspect of why Covid-19 is so infectious. You can spread it without knowing you have it, or before you have any symptoms at all. In future chapters, we will see how that affects our ability to eradicate Covid-19, which give us an indication of what the next few years shall bring.

There is one more important question to consider: might prior non-Covid-19 coronavirus infections affect subsequent infections in the same person? Yes, for sure. That is, if you have had the common cold recently, you might be protected from illness or death when you get SARS-CoV-2. We see such disease modification with influenza vaccines. Even if you still get influenza after you get a flu shot, you are less likely to wind up in the ICU or die from complications. Similarly, it may be the case that if you have, say, common cold coronavirus OC43 a couple months before you get Covd-19, you might not get as ill. The disease has been modified to be milder.

There is still a lot to learn, but it seems a common cold coronavirus may protect you from getting Covid-19. Or, if you do get it, maybe you won't be quite as ill. But even if there is cross-reactive immunity, and that immunity may be disease modifying, it doesn't last long.

5 REPRODUCTION NUMBERS AND HERD PROTECTION

There have been a lot of numbers thrown around during this pandemic, so I want to take time to understand a few of them. Numbers out of context rarely provide useful insights. If we can garner an understanding of the basics of viral replication, we can better understand why the models have been so inaccurate during this pandemic, and, perhaps, better understand the future of the pandemic.

One particularly insightful number is R naught (R_0). R_0 is also called the basic reproduction number, and it describes how contagious a virus is, given the behaviors of its host. It is not a biological constant. That is, R_0 depends on the interactions between the host (in this case, humans) and the virus. So-called non-pharmacological interventions such as sheltering in place, physical distancing, and mask use affect the R_0 as they lower viral transmission. For instance, early in the pandemic, before we understood how contagious Covid-19 is, we freely socialized and otherwise interacted with people. The R_0 in that situation is very high, as one person infects many others. As we decrease our interactions, fewer people are exposed, so the R_0 decreased. Those with asymptomatic infection who wear masks decrease the number of contagious particles in the air, decreasing transmission and thus R_0. The value of R_0 changes over time as host behaviors change. The virus is still equally as contagious, but our behaviors affect how it spreads.

R_0 assumes a fully susceptible, non-immune population. This is very important to understand. Early in a novel epidemic, no one has been exposed to the virus, and thus, there is no immunity in the population. As immunity builds in a population, R_0 becomes less useful, because immunity in a population decreases transmission. Immunity in the population is assumed to be zero when calculating R_0. For a truly novel virus, pre-existing immunity is unlikely. However, as we learned in the last chapter, there is some pre-existing or partial cross-reactive immunity to Covid-19 due to the endemic coronaviruses. The assumption that there was no pre-existing immunity to Covid-19 made initial R_0 calculations unreliable.

Thus, R_0 is useful early on in epidemics as it is directly corelated with the number of people who will get infected during the first wave. The campaign to "flatten the curve" was an attempt to decrease the R_0 and decrease the peak of the wave. The same proportion of people would get infected, just over a longer period of time, thus saving us from the crises arising from the shortage of ICU beds and ventilators.

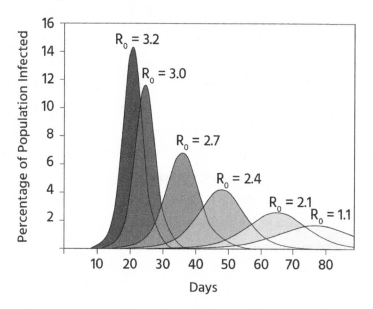

Source: Centers for Disease Control and Prevention

Above, you can see that the percentage of the population becomes infected depends on the R_0. A higher R_0 implies a greater and more rapid infection rate. In addition, R_0 also explains whether the epidemic is growing. If the R_0 value is greater than one, then the growth is exponential. The higher the number, the more rapidly you go up the exponential growth curve. If R_0 is less than one, then one person transmits the virus to fewer than one other person, causing the epidemic to die off. R_0 is generally calculated by seeing how many people an index case infects and then running models to estimate the number. In a mathematical world, we directly derive the herd immunity threshold from R_0.

Herd immunity threshold is the minimum percentage of infections needed to stop transmission in a population, which is calculated simply by $[1 - (1/R_0)]$. That is, take 1 and divide it by R_0, and then subtract that from 1. So, the higher the R_0 (the more contagious a virus is), the higher percentage herd immunity needs to be in order to stop transmission of the virus. That makes logical sense: something very contagious will transmit unless most people are immune. You stop exponential transmission by getting R_0 below 1. If we plug in 1 for R in the above equation, we get $[1 - (1/1)] = 0\%$. That is, you need 0% of people immune to the disease if you only transmit it to one other person. There is no exponential growth in that setting.

Getting R_0 below 1 breaks the back of the viral epidemic but does not stop all transmission. This is an important point to remember, and it will be discussed extensively in a later chapter. Let's look at the R_0 with a few different human diseases.

Disease	Transmission	R_0	HIT
Measles	Airborne	12–18	92–95%
Pertussis	Airborne Droplet	12–17	92–94%
Diphtheria	Saliva	6–7	83–86%
Rubella	Airborne Droplet	6–7	83–86%
Smallpox	Airborne Droplet	5–7	80–86%
Polio	Fecal-Oral Route	5–7	80–86%
Mumps	Airborne Droplet	4–7	75–86%
SARS	Airborne Droplet	2–5	50–80%
Ebola	Bodily Fluids	1.5–2.5	33–60%
Influenza	Airborne Droplet	1.5–1.8	33–44%

Source: Wikipedia

Above, you can see the higher the R_0, the higher the herd immunity threshold has to be in order to stop transmission. Measles is the most contagious in the examples above, with an R_0 in the double digits. Thus, more than 90% of a population must be immune to end a measles epidemic. On the bottom, the pandemic influenza is much less contagious and can burn out after about a third of people get it.

SARS has an R_0 of between 2–5, so somewhere between 50–80% of the population needs to be immune to this illness in order to prevent spreading of the disease. In the previous chapter, I mentioned that SARS was actually eliminated from human populations because we were able to control the spread. The R_0 of SARS is actually quite high, but remember, people did not become contagious until after they were already very ill. With SARS, simple infection control practices caused the R_0 to decrease from 2–5 to less than 1. Remember, R_0 is not a biological constant; it is the interaction between the virus and the host. If the host changes infection control practices, the R_0 changes as well.

The R_0 of COVID-19 is thought to be about 2.5–3, so initial projections are that 60–80% of the population will need to be exposed to this disease or effectively vaccinated before we stop the pandemic. This is a good place to start, but much more to come on the topic soon.

R_0 and herd immunity threshold both assume immunologically naïve populations. What happens once we start to get some folks exposed to the virus, and they survive and develop immunity? Let's learn about R_E, or $R_{Effective}$.

R_E takes immunity into account. The more immune folks you have in the population, the harder it is for a virus to spread. This makes sense, and R_E becomes the important number to consider once either the virus has significant penetrance in a population, or you have a vaccine.

R_E might be a better number to consider after you have passed through the first wave of the epidemic. The second wave will have an R_0 that depends on cultural practices of the host species (such as physical distancing and masks), but as more people become immune, R_E decreases more than the R_0.

The current reproductive rate in a community is expressed by the value R_T, or R_{Time}. R_T is the reproductive rate at the present time, with all factors that affect transmission of the virus in a community taken into account. This number is derived from a measurement of the amount of transmission. That is, if you look now at how many cases you had last week, and compare that with projections for next week, you'd be able to infer the R_T. If you are following websites that report on infection rates, this is likely R_T. With this number, you actually measure the attack rate, which is important information.

So, a brief summary: R_0 takes into account host effects (such as sheltering-in-place, physical distancing and masking when you cannot) but not immunity. R_E takes into account immunity due to prior infection or vaccination. R_T is an estimate of the actual current reproductive rate of the virus. Reaching the herd immunity threshold ends transmission of a disease in a population. It is calculated from the inverse of the virus/host interaction.

But that is not the whole story. There are other considerations in addition to the numbers above. So far, we have looked at how contagious the virus is, and what humans do socially to avoid it. In addition, there can be immunity (after disease or vaccination) that decreases transmission. These, when taken together, can signal when a truly vaccine-preventable respiratory disease (such as smallpox or measles) no longer transmits at all in a local population. Remember that Covid-19 is more complicated than that. First off, it is not truly vaccine preventable. That is, the vaccine doesn't work 100% of the time, and immunity is not long-lasting. And, there is asymptomatic transmission and a few other factors to consider.

We must look differently to understand herd immunity with Covid-19, because you can get it again. With smallpox or measles, once you get it, you are protected for life. The story of immunity and SARS-CoV-2 is much more complicated than what can be explained by R_0 and herd immunity. Other factors come in to play, such as asymptomatic infections, heterogeneous mixing, and partial non-specific immunity, which we will examine below.

Instead of R_0 or R_E, we need to be looking at the attack rate. Attack rate changes everything. It has to do with the number of secondary infections you get from an index case. It is another way to express the risk of getting an infection. Attack rate is expressed in whole numbers. If you have two people infected by the index case, the attack rate is two. It is calculated by taking the number of people who get the infection divided by the number who are at risk of getting the infection. Attack rate can be decreased by any number of reasons, including non-pharmaceutical interventions that affect R_0, immunity that affects R_E, selective heterogeneous mixing of different populations, and (most notably) partial non-specific pre-existing cross-reactive immunity.

Let's say that again: partial (it isn't fully protective all the time), non-specific (it isn't from prior Covid-19), pre-existing (it is present before SARS-CoV-2 was in populations), cross-reactive immunity (it provides some memory T-cell protection from Covid-19). This is not full immunity to Covid-19 (which may not even exist), but partial protection from a prior common cold coronavirus. So, say you get a non-Covid-19 coronavirus infection and have memory T-cells that cross react and prevent SARS-CoV-2 infection. This non-specific immunity decreases the attack rate but doesn't affect R_0 or R_E. Lowering the attack rate lowers the actual number of people who will get infected with Covid-19 in any population where SARS-CoV-2 is circulating.

Instead of herd immunity, we need to pay attention to herd protection. Herd protection is the threshold past which we break the back of epidemic transmission. Once herd protection is reached, regional communities stop having regional epidemics. It is the threshold you must pass in order to end the current wave of infection. In some respects, they are one and the same. In other instances, herd protection is used for describing, say, sanitation's effect on diarrheal disease or bed-nets reducing malaria. Sanitation and bed nets protect you from getting a disease in the first place rather than relying on immunity to prevent infection after exposure.

Remember, herd immunity threshold is simply the inverse of the R_0. It is intended for pandemic diseases that can be stopped through vaccination alone, like smallpox and measles. Covid-19 cannot be stopped by vaccination alone, similar to influenza. Herd protection, on the other hand, is affected by the number of people who get the disease, who get vaccinated, who have pre-existing immunity, and who are excluded by heterogeneous mixing of the population. It stops the epidemic transmission for now. It doesn't eradicate the disease. However, it marks the transition from regional epidemic to the next phase in this disease. I call this next phase the Transitional Phase, which is the subject of a later chapter.

Meanwhile, I glossed over another new idea: heterogeneous mixing of populations and the effect that has on attack rate and herd protection. I want to specifically mention heterogeneous mixing of populations, as there are folks who are going to get Covid-19 and those who are less likely to get it. Remember, there are still some people in the United States (and the world) who have not left their homes since the pandemic began. Others leave their home less than weekly. These people mix heterogeneously. That is, they don't mix, which lowers their risk of getting Covid-19. There are some adults, on the other hand, out at the beaches and bars, mixing it up. These (often) young folks have a high risk of getting the infection—and they will! If we were to split the population in half, we have those at higher risk of getting Covid-19 and those at lower risk. Once those at higher risk get it, they can't get it again for at least the next couple months. They remove themselves from the susceptible crowd and make spreading of disease more difficult. Yet the reclusive folks don't come out and take their place. Different populations don't mix randomly, as is the assumption with herd immunity.

Thus, heterogeneous mixing of the population lowers the attack rate but is not taken into account in most models of Covid-19 herd immunity. Social butterflies will become, at the very least, partially immune. Those who continue to isolate at home won't get Covid-19, which lowers the herd protection threshold. Numbers like R_0, and herd immunity derived from it, assume random mixing of people. We don't mix randomly, but rather with the same people over and over again. And some mix more than others. When we adjust for heterogeneous mixing, the herd protection threshold goes down even more.

Many in the public eye have been focusing on the wrong numbers. They have been looking at R_0 and imagining that 60–80% of people would need to get infected in order to reach herd immunity. Instead, we can look at attack rate and see that the back of the epidemic is broken at a much lower percentage of infections. Given heterogeneous mixing of the population, given asymptomatic infections, and given partial immunity, herd immunity is not the right goal. After all, we will never eradicate Covid-19. Herd protection is the goal. It may be that the herd protection threshold is as low as 10–20%. That is, after 10–20% of people in a region are infected, the epidemic wave may be over for now.

There is one additional factor that lowers the herd protection threshold. Let's get to know the black box.

6 THE BLACK BOX OF
NON-SUSCEPTIBLE PEOPLE

I mentioned earlier that even without pre-existing immunity from prior exposure to common cold coronaviruses, it seems that a segment of folks still doesn't get Covid-19 after exposure. That is, perhaps there are some people just not susceptible to Covid-19 infection.

This is the black box: Why, after exposure, do some people not get Covid-19? To begin to address this issue, let's review attack rate. Again, attack rate is the number of new cases in the population divided by the number of people *at risk*. But what does at risk mean? At first, it would seem correct to say that everyone is at risk of Covid-19 infection, since no human has interacted with this virus before. Apparently, however, not every human is at risk. In this setting, risk does not mean risk of morbidity or mortality once you have Covid-19. Rather, it is risk of becoming infected by Covid-19 in the first place.

The percentage of the population at risk certainly isn't 100%! We know this, because not everyone in a house tests positive after close family exposure. For instance, in a close-knit family, sometimes only 50% of family members ever test positive after an index case in that home. Further, you can have Covid-19 on a cruise or war ship, yet not everyone tests positive. We know just how contagious this virus is; it is very efficiently transmitted from person-to-person. So, why don't all exposed people wind up testing positive for Covid-19? Some folks are looking at the 60–80% attack rate in a closed setting (such as a ship or a prison) and using that as evidence that the herd immunity level is 60–80%. Most of the population doesn't live in those types of close quarters, so it's incorrect to view data this way and doesn't inform us as to the herd protection threshold outside the cruise and war ships. The real important question is: Why don't 100% of people get Covid-19 after significant exposure? Is this because people are resistant to getting Covid-19?

No. First, to an infectious disease physician, that is the wrong use of "resistant." We use the word resistant when talking about an organism. For instance, HIV and bacteria build up drug resistance, and they become resistant. However, being non-susceptible to an infection is different than being resistant. An organism can be or become resistant to treatment. A human, on the other hand, can be not susceptible to an infection. Specifically, that means for whatever reason, you don't get infected after exposure. Next, being non-susceptible isn't necessarily tied to immunity. There are rare folks who lack the cellular receptors that HIV uses to get into cells who do not get HIV. This is how bone marrow transplants have "cured" HIV. You can "give" someone these non-susceptible cells via bone marrow transplantation and make their HIV go away. Of course, bone marrow transplantations are complicated and extremely dangerous, which is why it is not a good way to cure HIV.

What about for Covid-19? Why do some people get exposed to SARS-CoV-2 and not get Covid-19? This is another way of asking the question of who is at risk for Covid-19. It represents the denominator in the attack rate ratio. Not everyone is at risk. In fact, depending on your age, you may be non-susceptible to Covid-19.

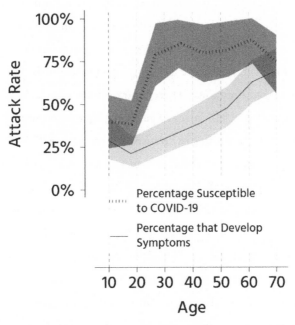

Above, you can see a figure from a paper in *Nature Medicine*,[2] which demonstrates the concept of non-susceptibility. This graph starts at age 10 and goes to age 70. Unfortunately, data wasn't collected for people younger or older.

The dotted line represents people who are not susceptible (above the line) or susceptible (below the line) to getting Covid-19. That is, after being exposed to someone with active Covid-19, above the dotted line you are non-susceptible, and below the line you are susceptible to getting Covid-19. Note that those who are young are mostly non-susceptible, but this rapidly

[2] Davies, N.G., Klepac, P., Liu, Y. *et al. Age-dependent effects in the transmission and control of COVID-19 epidemics.* Nature Medicine (26), 1205–11 (2020).

changes between 20–30 years of age. As people age, it remains steady that about 75% of the population is susceptible to Covid-19. So, at any age above about 30, about 25% of people are not susceptible to getting Covid-19 after exposure.

Next, the solid line shows those who go on to develop symptoms. The population above the solid line but below the dotted line represents the people asymptomatically infected after exposure. Those below the solid line represents those symptomatic from Covid-19. Note the slow, steady increase in this solid line. The proportion of people who develop symptoms after exposure goes up steadily with age. Still, at ages older than 70 there are still 25% of the population that are non-susceptible, with a small proportion who are asymptomatic, while about 75% of folks develop symptoms.

This is such an important concept, and with so many numbers. I want to simplify it and look at it again.

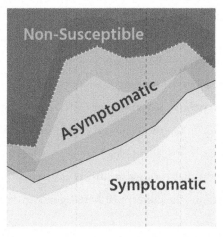

In the figure above, the people above the dotted line are non-susceptible to Covid-19 infection after exposure. This proportion of people changes rapidly at about 20-30 years of age. Prior to that, most are non-susceptible. After that, most are asymptomatic. But as people age, the chances that they are symptomatic rather than asymptomatic increase linearly.

These numbers are approximate and will evolve over time, but this is an important concept when considering age and attack rate. Under 20 year of age, the attack rate is about 20% after exposure. Over 70 years of age, the attack rate is 70% after exposure.

I would love to know the number in children younger than 10, as they represent a special at-risk group. Newborns have very different immune systems than even six-month-old babies, and that continues to change as they age. Although there have been outbreaks in daycares, in many places across the country, daycares never shut down. I would guess that there is a high percentage of children younger than 10 who are not susceptible to Covid-19. As for those over 70, it likely stays around the 25% range of non-susceptibility, but time will tell.

So, we understand that Covid-19 is very efficiently transmitted to people. If you have an infected person in a closed room, everyone in the room should get the infection unless they are immune or non-susceptible. However, who chooses (or is forced) to be in that room also affects transmission and attack rate and illustrates the concept of heterogeneous mixing.

What does it mean to be non-susceptible? I don't know.

That's why it is a black box. Why does it change with age? That's another good question! Some will consider it an entirely immunological phenomenon. That is, the immune system is responsible for not becoming infected after exposure, either due to past infection with coronaviruses or other infectious agents. I think the black box is a non-immunological process, meaning it depends on genetic expression. We know that certain people, depending on genetics and how their genetics are expressed in their particular environment, are more or less susceptible to a multitude of diseases. Even identical twins who share identical genes can respond differently to diseases depending on their environment. Some people will have small changes in either their genetic makeup or how their genes are expressed that cause them to be less susceptible to Covid-19 infection.

What is clear: Novel infections will have more variation in susceptibility than non-novel infections. That is, after an infection has been present in a population for a while, it has already had time to cause adverse effects on the population susceptible to it. Those most susceptible tend to get the disease and may die from it. Those less susceptible are less apt to get the disease and may become a greater share of the population. With a novel virus, the range of possibilities for susceptibility should be quite large before the population has been challenged with that infection. Later, as selective pressure is applied and some people depart the gene pool, susceptibility likely becomes more consistent across the population.

We can see the effect of past selective pressures from non-novel diseases in human populations. For instance, sickle cell and thalassemia traits are common in areas where malaria is endemic. As it turns out, these blood diseases protect people from dying after exposure to malaria. In pre-history, it is likely there was a wide range of susceptibility to malaria in the population prior to exposure. However, those with sickle cell and thalassemia traits survived malaria more often, and more frequently reproduced those genes in their children. Thus, these traits increased in the population. Similarly, it is thought that a single copy of a cystic fibrosis gene protects from death due to diarrheal illnesses. If you have one copy, you are more apt to survive and reproduce than those who don't have any copies. If you are unlucky and get two copies, you get cystic fibrosis, and unfortunately pass away at a young age. But the protection from a single copy outweighed the detriment from two copies. Thus, the cystic fibrosis gene became common in some populations where childhood death due to diarrhea was common.

Will we see Covid-19 change gene distributions in humans? Unlikely, given that advances of modern medicine decrease selective pressures. In addition, most who die from Covid-19 are past reproductive age, and thus won't pass on genes that are less or more protective. But it all depends on what is in the black box. Why are some people not susceptible to getting Covid-19 after significant exposure? I'm looking forward to the ebb and flow of scientific progress to provide an answer.

What is clear is that this black box further lowers the herd protection threshold. If some people, through genetics or genetic expression, are not susceptible to Covid-19 infection, the percentage of the population at risk (the denominator of the attack rate) is lowered. Thus, after exposure, fewer people get Covid-19 than predicted by models that don't account for the black box of non-susceptibility. This means that we will get to herd protection sooner than folks who talk about herd immunity predict. It is possible that after 10-20% of a regional population gets exposed to Covid-19, we have reached the herd protection threshold. At that point, the region moves into the Transitional Phase of the Covid-19 pandemic.

7 ERADICATION IS IMPOSSIBLE

Herd immunity is not the goal. Herd protection is. After all, eradication of Covid-19 is impossible, which means that there's no reason to attempt to get to herd immunity. Rather, we must stop epidemic transmission of Covid-19, which threatens our healthcare and public health resources. Once we get past the threat of regional epidemics, we move on to the Transitional Phase.

Covid-19 is a pandemic, which means it is made up of multiple simultaneous epidemics co-occurring around the globe. In the case of the United States, when we talk about Covid-19, people generally describe the pandemic either from a national or a state level. There can be "hot spots" in different parts of the country, which contribute to the total case count in the United States. Unfortunately, it is not terribly useful to look at the United States as a whole when discussing this epidemic. There is no epidemic in the United States. Rather, there are many regional epidemics. While it is true that we share common borders and limited resources to fight Covid-19, there is much too much regional variation to consider the pandemic nationally. Take, for instance, California, which has hundreds of urban areas and hundreds of thousands of acres of rural farmland. Compare California to New York City or New York State, and you have a false narrative.

Let's take a further step back and consider the case count of the entire world. While we share a common planet and resources, it is just not useful to consider massive areas as a homogenous epidemic. We must consider smaller subsets of the population when considering this pandemic.

I have found it most useful to consider the pandemic as co-occurring epidemics in specified regions. Generally, as health care and public health resources are regionally organized, epidemics should be considered regionally as well. Currently, American healthcare systems mostly operate independently, although regions can get help from either their state or the national government. This allows useful reporting of case numbers and targeted responses in a relatively homogeneous area. However, each region has different geography, population density, resources, and groups of vulnerable populations. Each will benefit differently from mitigation measures to control new infections.

Before we can even consider eradication of Covid-19, we must eliminate it from regions first—region by region. Elimination means eradication of a regional epidemic. Before we eradicate a pandemic, we must eradicate epidemic after epidemic.

It is said: think global, act local. In a pandemic, there are no truer words. While it is true that the rest of the world is just a plane ride away, we have to begin by thinking locally in order to manage the pandemic.

Let's dive in, then, and see how we can think about breaking the back of our regional epidemic. How can we get to herd protection regionally and end epidemic transmission in your part of the world? Remember, herd immunity is useful when discussing an epidemic that can be controlled in regional populations through vaccination. It is important to note that herd immunity, when complete, leads to the elimination of a virus regionally. If elimination is present in all parts of the world, you can eradicate a virus. This is what happened with smallpox and rinderpest, the only two diseases that we have actually managed to eradicate. These viral diseases are extinct in all populations, but still live frozen inside research and bioterrorism laboratories. We no longer need to vaccinate against smallpox in humans, because it has been eradicated from the world. Rinderpest is actually a disease in cattle and other ungulates that was eradicated through vaccination and surveillance.

More commonly, however, vaccination and herd immunity lead to the elimination of a virus. Rather than making a virus completely extinct or eradicated, elimination implies that the virus no longer circulates in a regional population. The virus, however, is still present in other human populations. Polio, measles, and mumps are examples of viral diseases that have been eliminated from highly vaccinated pockets of humans but are still present in populations where we cannot vaccinate enough people to get to local herd immunity.

Covid-19 is a different story altogether. With Covid-19, since immunity is neither long lasting nor complete, vaccination will not lead to local elimination or eradication. Even if we have effective vaccinations against SARS-CoV-2, we know immunity will wane and Covid-19 will continue to circulate regionally. Said another way, eradication of Covid-19 is impossible. With or without a vaccine, with or without effective treatment, Covid-19 will cause human disease indefinitely.

To demonstrate why eradication is impossible, let's look at the specific criteria for considering a disease eradicated. Eradication is defined as the permanent reduction to zero of the worldwide incidences of infection caused by a specific agent as a result of deliberate efforts. A virus that can be eradicated from humans must (1) not have non-human reservoirs, (2) be readily recognizable and have an effective treatment or vaccine, and (3) there must be worldwide desire and effort to eradicate the disease.

The first criterion is why MERS, also a coronavirus, will never be eradicated. MERS lives in camels, and we are unwilling to euthanize all camels in the world in order to eradicate MERS. Humans, however, are not preferred hosts for MERS. Although we are occasionally pinged with this highly deadly disease, we are mostly dead-end hosts for MERS. It does not readily transmit from human to human.

SARS-CoV-1 (which causes SARS) and SARS-Cov-2 (which causes Covid-19), on the other hand, both jumped species from bats. Neither are found in bats anymore, so we don't worry much about bats setting off another round of CoV-1 or CoV-2 again. However, note the nomenclature: 1, 2... What comes next? There are lots of bats and other species that carry non-human coronaviruses and may jump species, starting additional pandemics. But that is a different story.

With SARS-CoV-2, there may not actually be non-human reservoirs of this virus. Of course, cats, dogs, lions, tigers, alpacas and mink have all been diagnosed with Covid-19. But hopefully these are dead-end hosts (like humans are for MERS) rather than potential reservoirs.

Covid-19 probably could be eradicated based upon the first criterion of no non-human reservoir species. However, eradication requires both an effective treatment/preventative measure and easy recognizability. In addition, eradication of a disease requires worldwide desire and effort. Covid-19 fails both of these last two criteria, as will be discussed below. SARS-CoV-

1 and smallpox provide insight as to why we cannot eradicate SARS-CoV-2.

SARS-CoV-1, the virus that causes SARS, has been eliminated from human populations. However, it has not been formally declared as eradicated because there remains the concern of intentional or unintentional release of the SARS virus from laboratories. Other than the deep freezers in biocontainment laboratories, SARS-CoV-1 likely has no current natural reservoir. SARS does not have a treatment or vaccine, but it is relatively easy to contain, as it only spreads once you are quite ill. In addition, if you are worried about seeing cases of SARS (as would be the case if there was a known release from a laboratory), it is relatively easy to diagnose. There is no asymptomatic or pre-symptomatic spread. Thus, there is no reservoir for SARS, so it's easy to diagnose and thus contain. Global coordination also helped the elimination from all human populations.

Smallpox, again, has been eradicated. It has no non-human reservoir and is easy to diagnose, as you can see the pox from across the room. In addition, there is an effective preventative measure (vaccination), and, after you've had the disease, you are immune (and usually scarred) for life. Smallpox checks all the boxes, and thus was eradicated.

Covid-19 fails the last two criteria for eradication. Not only is diagnosis difficult given asymptomatic and pre-symptomatic transmission, but also Covid-19 is clinically indistinguishable from a host of other respiratory tract infections. If someone shows up with fevers, chills and a cough, it could be one of 100 infectious or non-infectious problems that are identical without diagnostic testing. Even once we develop rapid, reliable, point-of-care tests for Covid-19, there is still asymptomatic and pre-symptomatic transmission to worry about. And currently, there is neither effective treatment nor adequate preventative measures.

It may be possible that we never find a truly effective treatment for Covid-19. Historically, we have not yet developed an effective treatment for a respiratory virus, let alone a treatment for an asymptomatic respiratory virus. There are drugs with modest effect against influenza, and these drugs work to prevent influenza prior to exposure as well. But how do you treat someone who is just colonized by SARS-CoV-1 (asymptomatically infected) but not ill from Covid-19? Is it possible to treat someone who is not sick? As discussed in Chapter 2, drugs are difficult to develop for viruses since they use your own cells to replicate. Medications tend to have side effects, which make them undesirable to use when you feel fine but have SARS-CoV-2 replicating in your nose and lungs. We certainly will develop additional drugs against Covid-19, but no one sees pharmaceuticals as a silver bullet.

As for vaccination, odds are high that we will have vaccinations to provoke immunity for most who choose to be vaccinated. It is unlikely, however, that we will develop a vaccine that provides complete and long-lasting immunity. None of the other human coronaviruses provoke permanent immunity, even after natural infection. Immunity is temporary, and just like common cold coronaviruses, re-infection is expected after a period of time. This is true after natural infection and likely will be true after immunization as well.

As for preventative measures, if we could all live in a bubble for six weeks, we could likely stop almost all transmission of Covid-19. Can you imagine a way to accomplish this feat everywhere, simultaneously, around the world for a six-week period? This is not a realistic possibility for such a contagious virus. In fact, SARS-CoV-2 can be found in immunocompromised people for weeks on end. Any ember left behind would re-ignite the conflagration once the bubble ended.

Let's do a thought experiment for a second. Assume we have a vaccine for Covid-19 that is 100% effective and lasts for at least two years. This is unlikely, as no vaccine is 100% effective. If we vaccinate every man, woman and child in the world within two years, we eradicate Covid-19.

What about those folks who refuse vaccination, or those who live in inaccessible areas of the world? This is why we have not eradicated hepatitis A, hepatitis B, polio, measles, mumps and rubella. All of these infections have a single host—humans. They can be eradicated, but they haven't been. Even if there is an effective treatment or vaccination, imagine distributing it simultaneously around the world, let alone getting folks in the United States vaccinated 100% of the time.

There are countries around the world that will have 100% compliance with mandatory vaccination. The United States is not one of them. Beyond that, time and time again, we have seen worldwide public health efforts stall when diseases have almost been eradicated. The final criterion for eradication of a virus from humans is that there must be worldwide desire and effort to eradicate the disease. Once Covid-19 stops being an epidemic in many parts of the world, will the world truly have such desire, when we have failed with all eradication efforts before? Aside from smallpox, which is deadly, easy to recognize, and leaves horrible scars if you do manage to survive, humans have not been able to finish what they start with world-wide eradication efforts.

Since we cannot eradicate Covid-19 based upon eradication criteria, it is clear to me that Covid-19 will continue to circulate in human populations. It will become endemic—present continuously in low amounts. Covid-19 as a pandemic will end, but it will not be eradicated. It will go from epidemic to endemic.

There's an example in our shared history where this has already happened. Now, let's look at the time in human history when a human coronavirus caused an epidemic and is now endemic.

8 HOW EPIDEMICS
BECOME ENDEMIC:
A HISTORY

In this chapter, we'll look at a historical example of a human coronavirus that already transitioned from epidemic to endemic, so that we can understand the implications on the current coronavirus pandemic. Are there similarities we can garner in the past that will inform how Covid-19 will behave in the future?

As a reminder, coronaviruses are a diverse group of large RNA viruses. Many animal species are infected by one or two coronaviruses, and they cause various respiratory and non-respiratory diseases. Coronaviruses co-evolve with their current species, and, for the most part, don't cause severe disease in their host. They have evolved to be benign and do not needlessly kill off their host.

There are four strains of coronavirus that circulate widely in humans and cause the common cold. At some point in our pre-scientific history, I postulate each of those viruses jumped species and caused epidemics in human populations before evolving to be more benign. After all, it is unlikely they all co-evolved with humans. More likely than not, at some point they jumped over from an animal species, caused an epidemic, and eventually settled down, learning to live with their new human host.

One current common cold coronavirus did this recently. This human coronavirus jumped the species barrier, caused an epidemic, and is currently co-evolving with humans as an endemic cold virus. Meet HCoV-OC43. That's human coronavirus strain OC43. We'll call it OC43.

OC43 already caused an epidemic in human history and now is endemic, meaning that it circulates year-round in daycares and causes the common cold. 0C43 is one of the four common types of human coronaviruses that we can detect on multiplex molecular testing and is common in children who can be asymptomatic or have something as minor as a runny nose. A multiplex molecular test for respiratory viruses is now routine in hospitals, if not expensive. Kids—especially those in daycare—are germ factories! Children have 6–12 colds a year on average. First-time parents with children in daycare suffer greatly, but this suffering diminishes with subsequent children. Exposure to most of these cold viruses provides partial, short-term immunity. Consequently, parents and their children don't get quite as sick the next time they get the virus, and the immunity lasts about one or two years.

We can look at OC43's genetic code and see how different it is from its ancestor. Since we know approximately how many mutations occur randomly over time, we can date when OC43 made the jump from cattle to humans. That's right: humans have had at least one coronavirus epidemic before, and instead of bats it came from cows. It happened around the late 1800s when OC43 jumped from cattle into humans, presumably caused an epidemic, and eventually evolved into a strain which now causes the common cold.

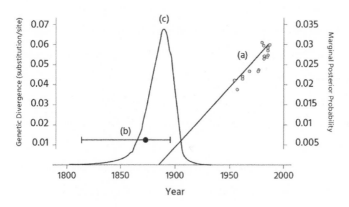

Above is a figure from a molecular clock analysis, which illustrates three estimates of when OC43 made the species jump.[3] These estimates are based upon genetic mutations that happen sporadically over time; they are essentially a genetic clock. If we know what the ancestor virus looks like in the native animal (cows in this case), we can see how different the virus looks now in humans as a way to guesstimate how long ago the virus diverged within each species. The time covered is from 1800 to 2000.

Line (a) is a type of analysis called linear regression. It crosses the x-axis at about 1890, which is the date that this analysis predicts the zoonotic event occurred. Line (b) is a maximum-likelihood estimate (the dot) with confidence intervals (the bars). The maximum-likelihood estimate postulates that 1870 was the year the virus most likely made the jump, with possible years ranging from 1810 to 1900. Curve (c) is something called a marginal posterior probability analysis, which simulates a bell curve distribution. This mode of analysis most likely places the jump at 1890, although 1860 to 1910 are within two standard deviations. The important point is not to understand the statistical or genetic analysis, but that three separate models all predict that a cow coronavirus jumped to humans around the same time.

So, according to the graph above, somewhere between 1810 and 1910, we have evidence that OC43 jumped the species

---

[3] Keyaerts L.V. *et al. Complete Genomic Sequence of Human Coronavirus OC43: Molecular Clock Analysis Suggests a Relatively Recent Zoonotic Coronavirus Transmission Event.* Journal of Virology. 79 (3): 1595–1604. 2005.

barrier. There were two particularly notable pandemics around that time, occurring in 1889 and 1918. Of course, 1918 is the year of the original horrific H1N1 pandemic. Swine flu in 2009 was the same H1N1 that re-visited humans and caused another milder pandemic. Luckily, for yet unknown reasons, H1N1 was less malignant in 2009 than in 1918. The pandemic in 1889 was most likely an H3 strain according to blood antibody tests that were kept from those who survived the 1889 pandemic.

So, if the pandemics of 1918 and 1889 are taken by H1 and H3, respectively, what other influenza outbreaks (it was all called influenza, the flu, or La Grippe back then) might be our friend OC43? Remember, aside from the above pandemics, it is impossible to distinguish influenza from coronavirus historically, so an outbreak may have been either virus, or in fact, any number of other respiratory viruses.

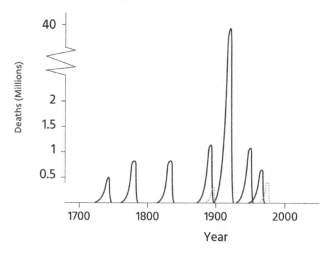

The figure above shows the history of pandemics and the

years they occurred between 1700 and 2000.[4] Look at the H1N1 influenza in 1918 with an estimated 40–50 million deaths; the scale for the rest of the pandemics was less than 1 million deaths. Next, you can see the peak to its left. This is the H3 Influenza pandemic of 1889.

There are many candidate pandemics above that are not the known influenza pandemics of 1889 and 1918. Might one of these be an OC43 coronavirus pandemic? In 1729, there was a three-year pandemic with progressively worsening waves (like in 1918), but that is too early to be coronavirus according to our timeline. In 1781, there was another pandemic that spread over much of Europe in eight months, with a high attack rate on the young. Also too early! Next up, the pandemic of 1830. This is our first candidate pandemic for coronavirus, as it falls well within the error bars of our molecular clock analysis. This pandemic spread for three years and was noted to have a very high attack rate with a relatively low mortality rate.

After 1830, there was a long break until 1889 (which was an H3 outbreak), and then our next candidate is the 1900 pandemic (the small dotted curve just overlapping the 1889 pandemic). But wait, was OC43 *necessarily* a pandemic? Maybe OC43 was just an epidemic, not a pandemic. As seen in Figure 2, there is a long period of time where there were no recorded influenza pandemics. What about epidemics?

---

[4] Potter, C.W. *A History of Influenza*. Journal of Applied Microbiology. (91) 572–79. 2001.

According to *The Chronicle of Influenza Epidemics*, [5] there were two influenza epidemics around the appropriate time. The first, called "the great influenza of 1847" in Britain, supposedly started in Russia. It spread to Europe, North America, and Brazil, and sickened between a quarter and half of people in Paris. Next, an epidemic that supposedly began in Panama in August 1857 that was referred to as "one of the greatest epidemics" swept through Rome. These two epidemics did not meet the criteria for pandemics as they were not widespread around the world. Is it possible that OC43 just caused an epidemic when it jumped species rather than a pandemic? As we know, zoonotic coronavirus infections can have very different infection rates and lethality. For instance, both SARS and MERS are more lethal than Covid-19 but also much less infectious. If the OC43 epidemic had different qualities (which it almost certainly did), it may have caused a different historical illness. Possibly there was localized epidemic, and then a subsequent endemic spread throughout the rest of the world.

However, we have yet to explore the 1899 epidemic. The "influenza" epidemic of 1899 is quite well known in influenza circles, because it was, until recently, thought to be the source of the H3 influenza. Many older textbooks claim that 1889 was when the H2 emerged and 1899 was when the H3 came to be. Using blood stored from the early 1900's, however, a re-

---

[5] Beveridge, W. *The Chronicle of Influenza Epidemics.* History and Philosophy of the Life Sciences. (13) 223–4. 1991.

interpretation of the data clarifies that the pandemic of 1889 was due to H3 influenza. [6] H2 did not cause either outbreak. So, what caused the 1899 epidemic?

In October 1899, the Queensland, Australia newspaper *The Capricornian* chronicled the beginning of an epidemic, writing:

> They appear to have made a severe attack on the citizens… and have not yet been repelled, but are marching on to further conquests… Still more recently they made an onslaught on the Government Printing Office, and drove so many of the staff to their homes that work has fallen into arrears. Influenza is not to be trifled with. [7]

Could this have been OC43? Yes!

So, what epidemic unleashed OC43 on the world? Was it 1899? 1830? Or maybe 1847 or 1857? I reproduce both a primary resource and a summary of these epidemics just to show you how hard it is to be a disease detective of the past. There are no more blood tests we can run from folks in that era. Unless we find more bodies in the permafrost, we will likely never know. I think it is very probable, however, that OC43 caused a local epidemic that either died out due to a high mortality rate (which is unlikely, because then it would be more like SARS or MERS and not endemic today), or had an acceptably low mortality rate such that it passed from cows to humans and is now a cause of the common cold.

---

[6] Dowdle W. R. *Influenza: A Virus Recycling Revisited*. Bulletin of the World Health Organization. (77) 820–8. 1999.

[7] https://trove.nla.gov.au/newspaper/article/68195375

Will the same will happen with Covid-19? That is, does Covid-19 have a low enough mortality rate and yet is contagious enough that it will continue to spread in humans and become the common cold? Given partial immunity with prior infection and the high likelihood that you will have Covid-19 multiple times, I think so.

Since we cannot eradicate Covid-19 and we have evidence that it will become endemic, the question is: What happens in between? After it is no longer an epidemic, but before it becomes endemic, we enter the Transitional Phase.

9 THE TRANSITIONAL PHASE

Covid-19 will become a common cold coronavirus but is currently a pandemic. A period of time sits between these two events, as SARS-CoV-19 transitions from one phase to the other. I am coining this period the Transitional Phase. This is the period in time after Covid-19 is no longer pandemic but before it is endemic and a fully understood medical entity. After a region has reached the herd protection threshold, epidemic transmission becomes ends, but cases do not go away. Cases of Covid-19 will never go away. They will transform into less frequent, less virulent, cold-like illnesses.

There is no specific event or number that signifies the

beginning or the end of the Transitional Phase. There won't be trumpets or an announcement to tell you that your community has reached it. The transition will be gradual. One can imagine significant community vaccination as a possible precipitating event, as it increases immunity levels in the population to some extent. But over time, gradually, the very nature of disease transmission will change in your region. No longer are there significant spikes in cases, but rather smaller, more contained stochastic transmission events will occur. The virus will still be present, but there are fewer susceptible folks and no more exponential growth. Certainly, there will still be mini clusters in smaller groups, but these sparks will no longer cause massive fires. As the R_T gradually drops below one, cases become mostly asymptomatic upon second and third exposure. As immunity in a population wanes over time, Covid-19 will cause outbreaks of the common cold in daycares. Covid-19 will act just like the other common cold coronaviruses do. When it becomes the fifth common cold coronavirus, the Transitional Phase ends.

Unfortunately, during the Transitional Phase, people will continue to die from Covid-19. As cases still occur, they will occasionally get to a vulnerable person and cause severe illness or death. There are presently pockets of people cloistered away from exposure to Covid-19. There will be those who, even with vaccination, remain susceptible to getting Covid-19 and will die from it. Death from a pandemic is a difficult thing to talk about. When it comes to Covid-19, we may be numb about death rates until it hits close to home. Then, a single case is too much.

Covid-19 will affect different families differently. A debilitating illness can change a family, and a single death of a child can devastate an entire community. During the Transitional Phase, loved ones, friends, and neighbors will continue to succumb to Covid-19. Mortality and morbidity will continue; this is an inevitable fact of a zoonotic pandemic in a world that hasn't planned for one in over 100 years.

I want to be sympathetic to those who have lost love ones. It is heart wrenching to lose someone, particularly when conditions prohibit you from being next to that person during the final days. It is clear when it comes to the Transitional Phase, however, that there are no risk-free choices. We cannot eradicate this virus, and we cannot close down the world. This virus is like water and will find cracks in a bucket. If we close down the world, this virus will find a way, and we will continue to face not only Covid-19 but also the negative unintended consequences of extended closures. There are no risk-free choices.

We know children must go to school, sports must be played, and businesses must reopen. The world will go on. And yet, so will the virus. During the Transitional Phase, we will learn how to navigate the uncertainties after reaching the herd protection threshold, keeping the risk of death from the virus in mind. I predict it will be 2–5 years before the Transitional Phase ends and Covid-19 is merely a cause of the common cold. I don't believe that we can have a full accounting for Covid-19 until that point, when everyone will have had the virus or been vaccinated several times, and those at highest risk will have died. We will not know whose plan "worked" and who did "good or bad" until we are past the Transitional Phase. Case counts and mortality rates only matter over longer periods of time, so for now, we need to keep looking at the data while always keeping in mind that new cases will occur.

I see two pathways for Covid-19 to transform into a common cold coronavirus. Either SARS-CoV-2 will evolve (when the predominant strain present changes), or prior infection and vaccine-derived immunity will mitigate the severity of infection. Let's look at each option.

There is a relatively uncommon idea in medicine that infections evolve to become better adapted to the hosts in which they live. That is, they evolve to be more benign. This is by no means a necessary function of a virus. The goal of a virus is, after all, to make as many copies of itself as possible in order to spread. If the virus can be more effective at spreading by being malignant, it will do so. Depending on the environment in which the virus lives and its mechanism of spread, it might evolve to be more benign. Imagine for a second that there are two competing strains of virus in a population. One kills off its host before it spreads, and the other is much more benign but more efficient at spreading. Over time, which version will you see more of? While we know there are different strains of Covid-19 already present in the world, it is unclear what effect, if any, these strains have on mortality or effectiveness of transmission. All things being equal, we will see the strains emerge that are the most successful at spreading, regardless of effect on mortality. This is evolution in action—the change over time of the strains that make up the population of a virus. Different stains have different genetic makeups, and thus genes change in the population.

This viral evolution is seen in real life late last century when HIV evolved to be more benign. HIV is truly a cunning virus, as it lives inside people for a variable period of time before causing symptoms. Yet, it can spread while the host is asymptomatic. If one strain of the virus killed its host early, how would that spread compare to one with a long period of asymptomatic illness? HIV killed people rapidly when it was first detected, and now, perhaps, more strains take a longer time to cause symptoms. HIV has evolved to be more benign now compared to when it first jumped species into humans.

So, too, may be the case with SARS-CoV-2. If there are strains out there that kill people rapidly, we should aggressively isolate, quarantine, and contact trace those cases. Conversely, if there is a strain that only causes mild disease in people, we are better off ignoring those cases. I believe that in order to help Covid-19 evolve to be more benign, we should not actively go looking for asymptomatic cases. Let asymptomatic Covid-19 spread and cause more asymptomatic infections. Asymptomatic infections may be a harbinger of a more benign virus. The difficulty here, of course, is that an asymptomatic strain may be a lethal strain that is only asymptomatic in its current host. Pass it on to grandma or an uncle with an organ transplant, however, and it may be a totally different story.

All things being equal, we need to be more aggressive with our control efforts for lethal or severe cases of Covid-19, and less aggressive with benign cases. If there are different strains out there, natural selection encouraged by behavior will allow the virus to evolve toward benignity. Our selective testing and isolation and quarantine strategies will shift the proportion of strains toward the gentler versions, more like the common cold. Yes, human behavior can help Covid-19 evolve to be less malignant.

Our immune system also plays a role in modifying the severity of disease. That is, once you have had an infection once, the second time may not be as bad as the first. This is a well-known phenomenon with certain diseases such as influenza. The second time you get a strain of influenza, you are not as sick as the first time you get it. If you get the influenza vaccine, even if it doesn't "work" and you get influenza, hopefully you don't get as sick. Instead of dying from it, maybe you wind up in the ICU. Or maybe instead of the ICU, you just need oxygen. The disease has been modified—it is not as bad. Through vaccination or prior infection, you prime the immune system so that it recognizes the virus and ramps up more quickly.

So, the first time you get Covid-19, it may be a severe illness lasting for weeks. As a result of exposure, you have now developed some immunity against Covid-19. The second time you get it, even though you may no longer have detectable antibodies, your memory T-Cells jump into action. Since you are primed to respond against an additional viral challenge, your immune system attenuates the course of the disease. The second time you get Covid-19, it will be less severe, and the third time you get it, maybe it'll be the common cold. Hopefully Covid-19 vaccines will be disease modifying as well.

How long will it take for Covid-19 to become the common cold? That is, how long will the Transitional Phase last? I estimate the Transitional Phase will last between two to five years. This gross estimate is based upon the idea is that it will take two to five years for most people to be exposed to Covid-19 more than once or twice. The second time you get it, you might not be as ill as the first time. By the third time, symptoms should be similar to that of the common cold, or maybe you will be asymptomatic. I am not basing this two-to-five-year time period on any fancy models, as we have seen too often how garbage-in-garbage-out models don't really predict the future. As commonly said, all models are wrong, but some are useful. Frankly, I don't know how long the Transitional Phase will last. It is, however, important to correct the common misconception that a vaccine will end the pandemic. It won't. Cases and deaths will continue with or without a vaccine, but gradually taper off over time.

Vaccines may affect how long the transitional period lasts. Vaccines sow some amount of immunity into the population and may actually shorten the time to reaching herd protection. If we get an effective vaccination, we will more rapidly move past regional epidemics and into the Transitional Phase. Perhaps, instead of being infected two to three times, some will be vaccinated two to three times, which will shorten the Transitional Period. An effective vaccine may help us get to and through the Transitional Phase, but it will not eradicate Covid-19.

In addition to ongoing deaths, I expect people will be hospitalized with Covid-19 even beyond the Transitional Phase. We still get occasional hospitalizations due to the endemic coronaviruses, especially in people with poor immune systems or those with cardiac or pulmonary conditions. As the Transitional Period wears on, we should see the number of hospitalizations decrease.

Also, as the Transition Phase progresses, people can begin to revert back to pre-pandemic cultural practices. Controlling R_T through cultural practices such as distancing and mask use are important during the Transitional Phase. This means that we cannot reopen everything and revert entirely back to the "old normal." Likely we will start with reduced physical distancing around those people we interact with the most. It is hard to foresee any large crowds gathering any time soon, however. Not, at least, with some risks attached.

Part of the great mask debate has revolved around the question of droplet versus airborne transmission. It is pretty clear there are times that SARS-CoV-2 is spread via airborne routes. Once there is an adequate supply of N-95 masks, expect to see these instead of bandanas as the facial covering of choice. Masks will remain an important accoutrement for the next several years. As a health care worker, I expect I will be wearing an N-95 mask for much of the rest of my clinical days. Just like HIV caused the advent of Standard Precautions, Covid-19 will provoke Respiratory Precautions. Standard Precautions requires healthcare works to wear gloves and other barriers when coming into contact with other people's bodily fluids. It is funny to think of a time technicians drew blood, or doctors stuck their fingers in people's mouths without gloves on. However, there were plenty of people reluctant to wear gloves when Standard Precautions began after the HIV epidemic. In the same vein, especially during respiratory season, health care providers will be wearing N-95s and eye protection. Actually, we were supposed to be doing that anyway, but enforcement was lax before Covid-19.

During the Transitional Phase, those more likely to get Covid-19 will still get it. Those more likely to die will, unfortunately, still continue to die. It will remain a problem for those unsheltered, those forced into shelters (jails, prisons, other high-density living settings), and for those who face social and economic disadvantage. Our communities will continue to adapt to these changes. Flexibility will be necessary as we try to balance relaxing the new normal and reverting to the old normal.

In summary, there is a period, what I'm coining the Transitional Phase, that will be shorter in some communities and longer in others. During this phase, there is enough herd protection that we no longer have to worry about overwhelming health care and public health systems with infections, but infections will still happen. There will be smaller clusters. There will be headlines in the news of ongoing tragedies, but these will become less frequent over time. Distancing rules will relax, starting at the family level, and ending with large crowds.

Eventually, most people will have seen this virus multiple times and have some relative immunity. SARS-CoV-2 will then become the fifth endemic human coronavirus. Occasionally it will pop up on a lab test, causing viral pneumonia or COPD exacerbation. It will be a known entity medically, and the world will move on. Meanwhile, how do we live with covid in the world?

10 HOW TO LIVE WITH COVID IN THE WORLD

In summary, Covid-19 is a novel, pandemic zoonosis that jumped from bats to humans in late 2019. The disease Covid-19 will become more benign over time, though the virus SARS-CoV-2 will be with humans for a long while. That is, while Covid-19 may become the common cold, we cannot eradicate this virus.

We can look to influenza pandemics, other human coronaviruses, and evolutionary biology for guidance about the future. As for influenza, there has not been a true pandemic for over 100 years. Much has changed in the world since 1918.

Pandemic influenza, however, establishes how a novel virus causes a worldwide catastrophe then circulates endemically after humans build some immunity to the new strain. We also can learn from the two failed pandemic strains of coronavirus, SARS and MERS. These human coronaviruses are lethal but not very contagious. After jumping from bats to humans, they were effectively contained. Because of their ease of identification, human-to-human transmission can be prevented by isolation and quarantine.

Circulating common cold coronaviruses help to understand virus-host interactions. These endemic cold viruses are not lethal but very contagious, and they reveal the expected effects of treatments and vaccinations for Covid-19. Finally, evolutionary biology provides a framework to understand the goals of a virus and how humans ought to respond to this pandemic.

Historically, we see with HCoV-OC43 that it is the destiny of SARS-CoV-2 to become the common cold. With or without a vaccine, with or without an effective treatment, we cannot eradicate this virus. It may evolve to be more benign, but more likely than that, our own immune system will provide partial protection after repeat infection, either naturally or through vaccination. SARS-CoV-2 does not meet the criteria to be considered for eradication; thus, humans must learn to live with Covid-19.

So, how to live with Covid in the world? Now is the time to get comfortable with and understand Covid-19. Now is the time to truly know our enemy. Now, let's call it "covid" with no capital letters or silly "-19." After all, Covid-19 is a stupid name.

While there is still much to learn about covid, the scientific process grinds forward in fits and starts. We must go on with our lives at some point. I'm not suggesting our lives will return to a pre-pandemic normal, rather a new normal. Or, as some have said, a new abnormal. After all, the world is in flux and changing all the time anyway, yet that change happens on a new timeline now due to covid. What do we need to understand in order to proceed with the new abnormal?

First, understand that every human will eventually be exposed to SARS-CoV-2. Someone will sneeze or cough on you, or you will otherwise breathe it in or transfer it to your mucous membranes. It will happen. Will you have pre-existing immunity from a prior cross-reactive viral exposure? Will you, for reasons not currently understood, have some individual characteristics that make you non-susceptible to becoming infected? Will you be vaccinated and thus primed to repel infection? Or will you have been exposed before, and thus have a milder case the second (and third) time? Understand, a plan to never come into contact with SARS-CoV-2 is not realistic. At some point, you will be challenged to defend yourself from this virus that wants to use you to make more of it. So, what can you do? Since you don't know if you are susceptible to a first or a second infection, you must do what you can to improve your overall health. That is not a medical recommendation, but common sense. Next, when vaccinations become available, it might make a lot of sense to get vaccinated if you are elderly or otherwise at risk for mortality or morbidity due to covid. Further, if you work with or visit vulnerable populations, it also makes sense to get vaccinated. While not a silver bullet against this vampire virus, hopefully vaccines will provide some protection from infection. And if not, hopefully they will at least modify the disease to make the symptoms more benign. That means you won't get quite so sick when you get covid.

Beyond vaccination, it makes a lot of sense to modify behaviors so that you reduce the probability of random interactions with covid. Yes, you need to live your life. And, yes, you will get covid, but perhaps not any time soon. After all, the more we learn about the virus, the better off you are likely to be. Plan on getting covid, but later. Not now. For a while, it is unlikely medications will be a silver bullet either. We are still learning about the possible long-term negative effects of covid. Perhaps there will be some better options for treatment in the future.

When trying to avoid covid, understand there are no risk-free options. Rural folks are likely to die in car wrecks, yet we choose to drive. Smokers know they increase their risk of cancer and COPD, yet they choose to smoke. Certainly, you can reduce the risk of cancer and COPD by just not smoking, but you have no similar option when it comes to covid. You can't choose to not get it. If you interact with other people, you are at risk. Period. But what can you do to minimize the risk while you maximize doing what is important to you? After all, at the end of shelter-in-place orders, we moved from obligatory public health mandates to individual risk-based decisions. In the United States, at least, you are free to choose how you interact with society, for the most part, anyway. Choose to do what is important to you and understand how to mitigate the risk of infection.

I think there are two things we need remember when living with covid in the world. The first is community suppression. Next, we must protect the vulnerable.

These two steps are simple but obviously not easy. In order to accomplish them, we must ensure common sense in the new normal. People don't like change, and perhaps common sense is not all that common. However, if we understand there are no risk-free options, perhaps we can better judge the true risks of any activity. Additionally, these steps are community specific. What works in one region may not be ideal in another. Be mindful of your community, your region, state, and the global pandemic, but your role is to ensure you follow these simple steps in your community.

First, let's talk about community suppression. You, for the most part, can only control what is in front of you day to day. You can only respond to your environment: the new normal around you. While there are shifting policies and guidance, we have moved beyond containment and mitigation to suppression. Containment implies you can shut down all transmission. We cannot. Even if we do, asymptomatic travelers will bring the virus back into communities. Mitigation implies severe restrictions in order to reduce cases. This is flattening the curve with shelter-in-place orders with the goal of preventing the overwhelming of our hospitals and ICUs. Once we pass the herd protection threshold, mitigation is no longer necessary, but we cannot willy-nilly revert to normal life. That is, you must continue to distance from folks who don't live in your house. Continue to think about how many people you interact with daily and how much time you spend with them. The fundamental purpose of community suppression is keeping community transmission of covid low enough to limit outbreaks. This is true even once your community is past the herd protection threshold. Remember that suppression efforts are important to keep R_T low, and infections can spike if we forget our manners and practice poor covid hygiene. Community suppression actually means changing cultural practice. It implies common sense for the new world we live in. We must control the spread of the virus in the community by ensuring its members act sensibly in the new world. Rules and mandates melt away as community-specific common-sense measures for the new normal take root.

The second step is mitigating the devastation caused by this pandemic virus. Protecting the vulnerable is not only the right thing to do, but it also protects our communities, health care systems, and social services from being overwhelmed. How you interact with the vulnerable (or with others, if you are vulnerable yourself) in your world is within your control. Some think that vulnerable populations will be burnt through during the early months of this pandemic, and that only the general population will be left to bear the brunt of the subsequent waves. I expect, however, that we will be talking about protecting vulnerable populations from covid through the Transitional Phase and even when covid is endemic. Our job is to determine the people who are vulnerable in our lives and figure out what it takes to protect them. Some, such as the elderly and those living in congregate living communities, are easy to notice. Other groups are less noticeable, such as those with medical co-morbidities, those in group homes, the homeless, jail/prison populations, health care workers, first responders, and others who provide essential services. Finally, the most vulnerable are those most difficult to see, those at socioeconomic disadvantage. The Transitional Phase will be full of ongoing discussions about how to protect the vulnerable. If there is a silver lining from this pandemic, perhaps it will be around more equitable treatment for those who are hindered socially and economically.

People with symptoms must stay home. If you might be infectious, wear a mask if you cannot distance. Stay outdoors, or at least in well ventilated spaces. The common theme in these steps is that it is up to you! You cannot control the policies put in place around you, but you can control how you interact with the world. You can protect the vulnerable and do your part not to spread the virus. This is simple to do, but not easy to do all the time. And of course, you cannot control what other people do, just like we cannot always stop drunk drivers, school shootings, and many other potentially horrific events that may befall a community.

I want to end this short book on a positive note and tell you how this pandemic, and indeed all pandemics, will end. Before I do that, I'm going to place some blame, not on the virus, and not on the world that didn't prepare for a pandemic for the last 100 years, but on those most responsible for what a disaster the world's response to a pandemic has been. Who are those who have let us down the most during this pandemic? There are plenty of good people in all of these fields but equally plenty of examples in each where perverse incentives got in the way of doing the right thing.

The media. The media has been horrific, reporting on pain and suffering, trying to score points to prove others wrong, all in a thinly veiled attempt to sell advertising to eyeballs. If there was one group we would have been better off without during this pandemic, it would be the media.

Next, politicians. Politicians, by their very nature, make political decisions. This isn't a blame game on our current set of Republicans or Democrats, but rather an indictment on individual political decisions. Decisions have been based on an effort to score political points and get re-elected rather than doing what is right. While, most of the time, we didn't know exactly what the right thing to do was, it is clear people took sides as a result of partisan affiliation. The polarization of this quagmire brought the worst out in people and left common folks uncertain as to what to do.

Finally, scientists themselves are to blame. There has been such a rush to publish that most of what has been published is literally garbage. Indeed, there has been little responsibility by editors to control the onslaught of garbage. Even *The Journal of Middle Age Finger Art* has been publishing articles about the science of Covid-19 in a race to the bottom. This rush to publish has led to inaccurate scientific conclusions and lack of discussion about the quality of the evidence presented. These inaccurate conclusions are then used by politicians and news media to sow discord, in accordance with their mandates—for the politicians to get elected, for the news media to shock and awe, and for scientists to increase their citation scores. The response to this pandemic has shown that incentives truly matter. In a world where confirmation bias is a click away, a balanced and accurate message can become hastily muddled. When looking at a message, remember to try and understand what it is saying, and why the person is saying it. What is the incentive of the messenger?

Since we don't know what is ultimately going to happen, whom do you trust? I suggest you don't trust the national news media for your information. Ignore politicians and scientists as well. Think about who has incentives most aligned with your goals, and trust yourself. You have the individual responsibility to interact with covid in the world and take care of your family and community. While you may not understand the intricacies of the science, at least understand that all science changes over time with new knowledge. Read and hear both sides of an issue. Understand inherent biases and incentives. Ultimately, make your own decisions. It is a tall order for a world that would rather pop a pill than fix an underlying issue, but it is the only way to sus out the garbage.

Currently, we have an irresistible force pushing an immovable object. This is known as the *irresistible force paradox*. Pandemics, I believe, are an irresistible force of such destructive potential to push an immovable object—human ingenuity. This force is so irresistible that they must all be entirely eradicated in our lifetime. Don't bet against the most successful species that has conquered every challenge yet thrown our way. When was the last time humans faced such an irresistible force?

At least in the United States, the last time was World War II. Prior to the beginning of the War, the US was slow and clumsy. We watched what was going on overseas and did not ramp up for wartime production. Then, as now, we did not prepare. By the end of the War, however, we produced enough to overwhelm all enemies. Production became an irresistible force, enough to decimate any adversary. However, production did not win the war, human ingenuity did.

So, it will be with covid. Despite the great capacity of the American people and our industries, you cannot outproduce a virus! Production cannot increase exponentially. Equally as unlikely, we won't outwit the virus with a magical medicine. Since the beginning of time, we have only found a few medications that have any effect on viruses that cause respiratory tract disease. Nor will a vaccine win the day. Without a doubt, candidate vaccines will be produced and distributed around the world, but they won't eradicate this enemy. If we cannot stop influenza from killing our most vulnerable populations, then we will not stop covid with a vaccine.

Winston Churchill said, "You can depend upon the Americans to do the right thing. But only after they have exhausted every other possibility." You can depend on us to do the right thing. We will work to save lives and minimize morbidity. We will produce PPE for the entire world. We will make medicines and vaccines. We will produce. We will try everything possible. But the way the pandemic ends? Just how World War II ended.

World War II did not end with overproduction of known products. It ended with a paradigm shift: nuclear weapons. These weapons were not even a glimmer on the horizon in the beginning of the war. An innovation out of left field ended the conflict.

My prediction: something out of left field will end the covid pandemic. Something, someone, somewhere, has in the back of her mind will sprout and take form to decimate covid. After all, we have botanists, astrophysicists, zoologists, and everyone in between thinking about this problem. While I can't tell you what specifically will end the pandemic, since it won't be medication, vaccines, or production of PPE, it will be a novel idea. Just like nuclear bombs ended the war, an innovation we don't yet know will end covid. Something we can't even conceive of yet will emerge and end the scourge.

So, in the war of the irresistible force and the immovable object, do you want to be the force or the object? When you put the ingenuity of the humans to task, never doubt people to come to it. Right now, the end of covid is a thought in the back of someone's mind. Give it some time to germinate. The end of the pandemic is already out there, yet to be recognized.

Just as nuclear weapons ended all future World Wars, whatever stops covid will also end pandemics for the rest of time. I have faith that it will be just that revolutionary. Our generation will fight this pandemic. Future generations will look back and recognize the struggle. The outcome: humans win, and the innovation that ends this pandemic will prevent all future pandemics from ever taking seed.

ABOUT THE AUTHOR

David M. Graham, MD, is a practicing board-certified Infectious Diseases Physician. He lives in small town Montana surrounded by his family and too many animals. Contact Information at www.FiPhysician.com

Woodland Christmas

Woodland Christmas

FRANCES TYRRELL

Scholastic Canada Ltd.

Scholastic Canada Ltd.
123 Newkirk Road, Richmond Hill, Ontario, Canada L4C 3G5
Scholastic Inc.
555 Broadway, New York, NY 10012, USA
Scholastic Australia Pty Limited
PO Box 579, Gosford, NSW 2250, Australia
Scholastic New Zealand Limited
Private Bag 94407, Greenmount, Auckland, New Zealand
Scholastic Ltd.
Villiers House, Clarendon Avenue, Leamington Spa,
Warwickshire CV32 5PR, UK

The illustrations for this book were done in watercolour
on Arches rag paper.

This book was designed in QuarkXPress,
with type set in 20 point Galliard.

Canadian Cataloguing in Publication Data
Twelve days of Christmas (English folk song)
Woodland Christmas
ISBN 0-590-12390-4
1. Folk songs, English - England - Texts. 2. Christmas
music. I. Tyrrell, Frances, 1959- . II. Title
PZ8.3.T9 1997 j782.42'1723'0268 C97-930524-1

5 4 3 2 1   Printed and bound in Canada   7 8 9 /9

For our little cub, Neil.

The animals in this book are:
one gray partridge,
two rock doves, three ruffed grouse,
four common loons, five river otters,
six Canada geese, seven whistling swans, eight raccoons,
nine red foxes, ten moose, eleven red squirrels,
and twelve beavers.
The bird in the potted pear tree
is a California partridge,
and the courting couple are black bears.

On the first day of Christmas,
My true love gave to me
A partridge in a pear tree.

On the second day of Christmas,
My true love gave to me:
Two turtledoves
And a partridge in a pear tree.

On the third day of Christmas,
My true love gave to me:
Three French hens
Two turtledoves
And a partridge in a pear tree.

On the fourth day of Christmas,
My true love gave to me:
Four calling birds
Three French hens
Two turtledoves
And a partridge in a pear tree.

On the fifth day of Christmas,
My true love gave to me:
Five golden rings
Four calling birds
Three French hens
Two turtledoves
And a partridge in a pear tree.

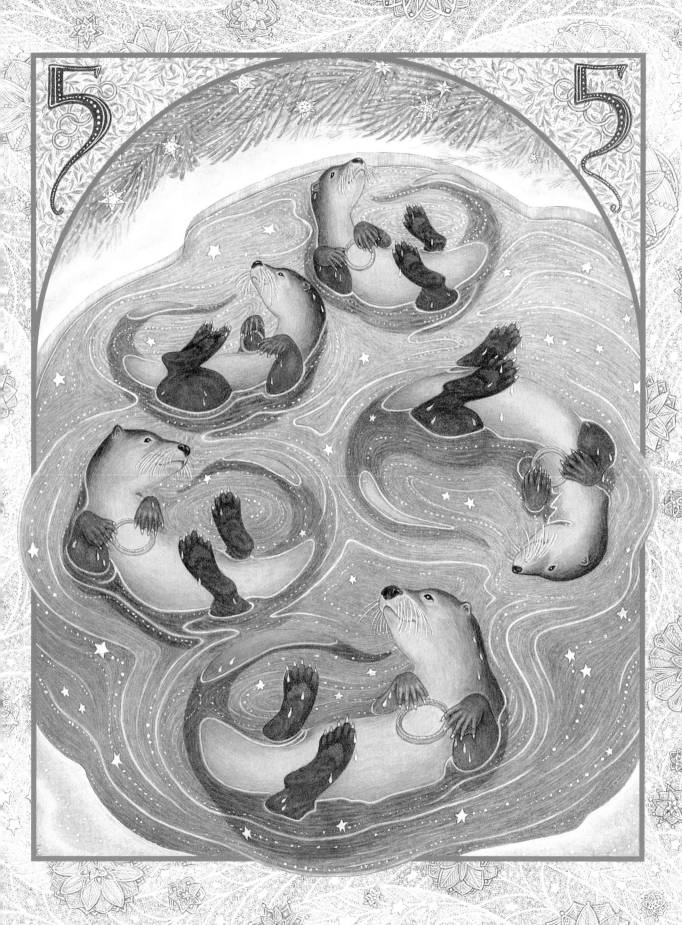

On the sixth day of Christmas,
My true love gave to me:
Six geese a-laying
Five golden rings
Four calling birds
Three French hens
Two turtledoves
And a partridge in a pear tree.

On the seventh day of Christmas,
My true love gave to me:
Seven swans a-swimming
Six geese a-laying
Five golden rings
Four calling birds
Three French hens
Two turtledoves
And a partridge in a pear tree.

On the eighth day of Christmas,
My true love gave to me:
Eight maids a-milking
Seven swans a-swimming
Six geese a-laying
Five golden rings
Four calling birds
Three French hens
Two turtledoves
And a partridge in a pear tree.

On the ninth day of Christmas,
My true love gave to me:
Nine ladies dancing
Eight maids a-milking
Seven swans a-swimming
Six geese a-laying
Five golden rings
Four calling birds
Three French hens
Two turtledoves
And a partridge in a pear tree.

On the tenth day of Christmas,
My true love gave to me:
Ten lords a-leaping
Nine ladies dancing
Eight maids a-milking
Seven swans a-swimming
Six geese a-laying
Five golden rings
Four calling birds
Three French hens
Two turtledoves
And a partridge in a pear tree.

On the eleventh day of Christmas,
My true love gave to me:
Eleven pipers piping
Ten lords a-leaping
Nine ladies dancing
Eight maids a-milking
Seven swans a-swimming
Six geese a-laying
Five golden rings
Four calling birds
Three French hens
Two turtledoves
And a partridge in a pear tree.

On the twelfth day of Christmas,
My true love gave to me:
Twelve drummers drumming
Eleven pipers piping
Ten lords a-leaping
Nine ladies dancing
Eight maids a-milking
Seven swans a-swimming
Six geese a-laying
Five golden rings
Four calling birds
Three French hens
Two turtledoves
And a partridge in a pear tree.

The
Twelve Days of Christmas

Moderately

On the first day of Christ - mas my true love gave to me A par - tridge _ in a pear

tree. 2. On the sec-ond
3. On the third   day of Christ - mas my   true love gave to   me
4. On the fourth

two tur-tle-doves,
three French hens.   And a
four call-ing birds,

(Repeat as needed)

par - tridge _ in a pear tree.   5. On the fifth day of Christ - mas my true love gave to me

D.S.

five gold - en rings, four _ call-ing birds, three French _ hens,

two _ tur-tle-doves, And a par - tridge _ in a pear tree.   6. On the sixth
7. On the sev-enth
8. On the eighth
9. On the ninth   day of Christ - mas my
10. On the tenth
11. On the elev-enth
12. On the twelfth

true love gave to me   Six geese a - lay - ing   five gold-en rings,
Sev-en swans a - swim-ming
Eight maids a - milk-ing
Nine la - dies danc-ing
Ten lords a - leap-ing
Elev-en pip-ers pip-ing
Twelve drum-mers drum-ming

four _ call-ing birds, three French hens,   two _ tur-tle-doves, And a par - tridge _ in a pear tree.